Dramatizing Writing

Reincorporating Delivery
in the Classroom

Dramatizing Writing

Reincorporating Delivery in the Classroom

Virginia Skinner-Linnenberg
North Central Michigan College

LEA LAWRENCE ERLBAUM ASSOCIATES, PUBLISHERS
1997 Mahwah, New Jersey   London

Lawrence Erlbaum Associates, Inc.
10 Industrial Avenue
Mahwah, New Jersey 07430-2262

Library of Congress Cataloging-in-Publication Data

Skinner-Linnenberg, Virginia.
Dramatizing Writing: reincorporating delivery in the
classroom/Virginia Skinner-Linnenberg
p. cm.
Includes bibliographical references and index.
ISBN 0-8058-2790-0 (alk. paper)
1. English language—Rhetoric—Study and Teaching—Activity programs. 2. Report writing—Study and
teaching (Higher)—Activity programs. 3. Debates and
debating. 4. Oral interpretation. 5. Drama in education.
6. Role playing. 7. Discussion. I. Title.
PE1404.S58 1997
808'.042'07—dc21   97-7495
                                                    CIP

Printed in the United States of America
10 9 8 7 6 5 4 3 2 1

Contents

Preface

Some years ago, while in my PhD program at Bowling Green State University, I mentioned to my friend and dissertation chair, Sue Carter Simmons, that I wanted to somehow combine my passions for rhetorical historiography and contemporary drama. She suggested I investigate the possibility of delivery in the composition classroom. As cliché as it may be, the rest was history. This text is the culmination of several years of research in the history and theory of delivery, as well as its uses as a strategy to aid writing students in their struggles.

I agree with John Frederick Reynolds when he states that the serious consideration of memory and delivery is long overdue. Their presence has always existed in some form in the composition class, yet attention to the theoretical basis for that presence has been conspicuously absent. If the rhetoric revival is to survive, as Reynolds writes, we must pay heed to the rhetorical canon as a whole. Although I have ignored memory, I present, in this text, applications of delivery for writing teachers. (Dealing with memory will have to wait until the next book.)

Of course, this text was not my effort alone. I have many people to thank for their support, guidance, and understanding, particularly Sue Carter Simmons. Without her encouragement and suggestions, this book would still be just a file in my computer. I would also like to thank the faculty of two different schools: Bowling Green University, who graciously responded to my requests for teaching methods, and North Central Michigan College, who gave me the final encouragement to see this book into print. In addition, my gratitude extends to Kathleen O'Malley and Nicole Bush of Lawrence Erlbaum Associates for their support and suggestions in the revisions of my text. I must also gratefully acknowledge my husband, Dan, for his undying love, encouragement, and understanding, especially on those warm summer days when he would stand at my office door and ask, "Can you come out to play?" and I would have to say, "No, I've got to finish this book."

Finally, this book is dedicated to my students, those people who have a wonderful impact on my life everyday. If I have the slightest positive influence on their lives as well, I am sincerely happy.

—*Ginny Linnenberg*

Introduction

Reintegrating Delivery to Writing

Voices are humming in the classroom. In each small group of students, someone reads an essay and other group members respond to the questions or comments of the author. The small group in the corner is animated. I edge closer to eavesdrop, as I so often do during these workshops.

"What do you plan to do on your next draft?" Valerie asks Paul, a question the students have learned from me. He has just told the group that he really doesn't like his description of his friend's mannerisms.

"Fix the wording, I guess. But I'm not sure how." He squints at the paper's typewritten words.

"Show us how he acts."

He thinks a moment and then pantomimes his friend's hand motions.

Valerie imitates what he has just done. "Okay. Now how would you describe what I'm doing?" She repeats the action.

Paul begins to describe her movements, at first in general terms, then in more detail.

She smiles and nods. "Say it just like that." The other two group members agree.

Paul returns her smile, grabs his pen and writes furiously, his problem of description solved.

Still the traditional writing classroom exists where the silence is only broken by the scratching of pens on paper and the droning of a lecturing teacher. However, more and more in contemporary writing classrooms, voices are replacing the silence. Workshops in which the students, as well as the teachers, exchange ideas about writing are more common. Teachers use debates, role-playing, and discussion to get students to analyze ideas and concepts before writing about them. Where did these traditions originate?

What reasons are there to break the silence that has smothered creativity in the writing classroom? Why have so many writing teachers tried to reincorporate voices and gestures into their classrooms? To answer such questions, we must trace writing instruction to its origin in classical rhetoric and define the influences at work in our contemporary classrooms.

Classical rhetoric divides the process of persuasive speech into five stages: invention, arrangement, style, memory, and delivery. Invention, arrangement, and style have historically received the most attention in traditional writing classes. On the other hand, *delivery*, the presenting of speech with effective gestures and vocal modulation, has often received rather perfunctory treatment, as did memory.[1] Yet, many of the ancient orators thought delivery to be necessary to rhetoric. They understood that voice, gesture, and facial expressions affected all the other stages of the speech.

By the eighteenth century, elocutionists recognized that delivery had an enormous power over an audience in rhetoric. Several orators, Thomas Sheridan and Gilbert Austin particularly, gave great attention to delivery, now combined with the larger area of elocution. However, by the nineteenth century, rhetorician Henry Day split elocution from vocal delivery. In higher education, due to competition from science and technology in the curricula, rhetoric was forced into one- or two-semester courses. By the late nineteenth and early twentieth centuries, composition became an adjunct subject in English literature departments, and a separate department of speech communication was formed to take over the instruction of delivery and the study of rhetorical history (Bizzell and Herzberg 13). This left invention, arrangement, and style for the composition classroom, thus dividing the classical five parts of a speech, a situation that continued until contemporary times; theorists now have slowly begun to view delivery and writing theory in a new light.

Likewise, going beyond vocal rhetoric to the realm of written discourse, I consider delivery to be just as important to the actual composing process of writers as it is to orators. And many contemporary theorists feel the same. For instance, Kathleen Welch writes that delivery is the site for uncovering trends in electronic forms of discourse ("Reconfiguring" 22). Furthermore, contemporary French feminists and critics Luce Iriguray and Helene Cixous

---

[1]Although I am discussing delivery in detail, I have also consciously ignored memory, the other part of Cicero's canon that was banished from writing classes. I also believe that memory is important to the five canons, but I also feel that memory is already used when writing. Students must dredge from memory not only what they will write, but also all the basic needs of writing: how to form sentences, words, letters, even simply how to hold a pen, or use a keyboard. Therefore, because I am concentrating on the reinstating of a physicality to writing, I leave the investigation of memory to another project. For a contemporary discussion of memory, see John Frederick Reynolds' *Rhetorical Memory and Delivery*.

believe that the feminine process of composing incorporates more of the body instead of merely the mind. Critic Michel Foucault encourages all writers to incorporate more of the body in writing. Part of that body in writing may be as simple as breaking the silence of the classroom through the use of voice. In fact, many theorists acclaim speaking and writing as integrated processes. Barry Kroll and James Moffett, for example, believe that oral and written resources are closely interwoven. Robert Ochsner determines that prose written in a speech-like style is much easier for the reader to interpret (88).

Nonetheless, because the rhetorical canon remained divided for so long, a contemporary bias against delivery in writing has led theorists to overlook this area of rhetoric and to undertheorize a variety of strategies that have been and could be used in teaching writing. My contention is that through the use of delivery, more and new strategies may be developed to aid in the teaching of writing. Thus, the overall focus of this text is the redefining of delivery for writing, its reunion with the other classical parts of the rhetorical canon, and its practical applications in the classroom.

Over the centuries, definitions of delivery have ranged from the purely physical to a more intellectual influence on the physical delivery. According to Cicero (*De Inventione*, Book I, VII, 9), who first established the five canons of rhetoric, delivery is "the control of voice and body in a manner suitable to the dignity of the subject matter and the style." In other words, for Cicero and many other classical rhetoricians, delivery provides the physical manner in which the orator communicates or conveys the text to an audience. Bacon, on the other hand, reinterprets delivery as "the means by which knowledge is used and incorporated into social institutions, which are maintained in memory" (Bizzell and Herzberg 624). For him, delivery takes on a more philosophical definition. Cicero, like other elocutionists, con-cludes that delivery is a physical act, done entirely with the body. Bacon, on the other hand, describes delivery as incorporating a more mental act along with the physical. He claims that delivery is not strictly using the body to reinforce meaning or persuasion, but, from his definition, Bacon seems to conclude that delivery is a culmination of the speaking or writing task, encompassing the exchange of text between the orator or writer and the audience. There is more of a social process implied here: the audience must use its knowledge to actively relate to what the orator or writer is stating in the text, and then the audience gains further knowledge, which is stored in the memory for future reference. For centuries, theorists have moved back and forth between these two definitions, creating a tension that eventually led to the split of delivery from the rest of the rhetorical canon.

Even so, I believe that all five elements of Cicero's classical canon, which provided a foundation for Bacon's concepts, have an impact on one another; they are hardly separable entities. I cannot write effectively without all the steps in the process. I may even suggest that there is a sixth canon, the whole person. If we were to fragment the whole, the rhetorical act inevitably suffers. Therefore, because all steps are necessary, I along with other contemporary theorists want to see delivery reestablished in its rightful place as an integral step in the composing process. Putting the *body*, the physical act, back into composition may restore the whole.

Although speech departments have owned delivery for the last one hundred years, those who teach writing, especially English departments, can gain a great deal by reinstating delivery into their conceptions of and theories about writing. Thus, in my vision of "dramatizing writing" in the composition classroom, delivery can have an impact on all the composing steps, from invention to final draft. A rough, basic outline of how this might work is:

- Using a play concerning a social issue to stimulate discussion in the classroom.
- Role-playing in small peer groups to debate issues.
- Brainstorming through performance of ideas for peer groups.
- Dramatic readings of drafts for peer groups' revision process.

In this type of application, Cicero's physical concept of delivery is not only present, but Bacon's social process of delivery is quite evident in the collaboration. The student, who may be writing an essay, enlists the aid of the peer group through delivery of the ideas and then the group interacts or dramatizes to present their input on the essay.

Although I believe that delivery needs to be reinstated in the writing classroom, I must also acknowledge the fact that delivery does already exist in many contemporary classrooms. As I stated earlier, for years, some teachers have used what I believe are delivery strategies as ways to get students to think about their writing. However, we have not had a theory to explain why we incorporated such performance in our writing classes. We have had theories on the connections between speaking and writing, theories on collaboration and audience, even theories culled from theater performance. Currently, we also have theories of delivery as computer-generated writing, the physical final product and its design. Nevertheless, writing theory has, for the most part, remained steeped in the mind and hands of the students, not in the whole body. That is, the purpose of this text is twofold: (a) to give writing teachers a theory behind the more physical, whole body, practices in the classroom; and (b) to outline many more practical applications of that theory. To this end, I have divided the text into three main parts: the first covers the history of delivery; the second discusses theories that contain facets of delivery from which I formulate my own theory of delivery; and the third discusses practical applications of my theory.

In chapter 1, I cover the history of the theory of rhetorical delivery by setting up a continuum that flows from a totally physical delivery to a noetic delivery, which incorporates more intellectual processes. My argument is that the tension between the theories at the two ends of this continuum led to the eventual division of the rhetorical canon. The chapter begins with the sophists and covers the periods of Classical, Medieval and Renaissance, the Elocutionary Movement, Neoclassical, and the Rise of Composition in the United States. To round out this history, I have also included a section on the more contemporary discussions of delivery. Furthermore, I incorporate here a separate discussion of The Women's Challenge to Delivery in the Rhetorical Tradition because, traditionally, there are very few women included in rhetorical studies (although that is changing) and it was difficult for me to find any women rhetoricians who specifically expounded a theory of delivery.

While chapter 1 gives the reader a basic context and definition of traditional delivery, chapter 2 provides insight into the state of delivery in contemporary approaches to writing instruction. We might say that it is the soul of the text. Because delivery was exiled from writing theory at the turn of the century, a modern bias has, for the most part, kept it from informing many contemporary theories. Therefore, as an answer to a variety of strategies that have been undertheorized, I have divided this chapter into discussions on theories of speaking and writing, dialogue (an umbrella for collaboration and audience), performance, and the feminist theories of "Writing the Body." The chapter culminates in my own synthesized theory of delivery, which incorporates facets from each of the chapter's divisions.

Finally, what good is theory without a means to apply it? If chapter 2 is the soul of the text, then chapter 3 is what might be called the body of the text. Here, I give teachers practical applications of delivery for their classrooms. Some suggestions are as simple as reading essays aloud, miming one emotion, posing for a few seconds to illustrate a thought or reaction, or projects as demanding as performing a play. The chapter is divided into sections of dramatizing voice alone, dramatizing body alone, and full physical performance, which is further subdivided by activities such as improvisation and role-playing.

As a writing teacher, I am always on the lookout for ways to help my students help themselves to write better. Ultimately, that is what I had in mind when I launched this project. Using drama to reincorporate delivery in the classroom will help students to utilize their bodies, as well as their minds, in their writing. In the long run, students will be given the tools to improve their writing long after their classes are over. With this in mind, I want to introduce delivery and its place in rhetorical history.

1

Delivery's Place in Rhetorical History

Through rhetorical history, delivery has moved back and forth between two extremes. At one end of the continuum, delivery is conceived of as totally physical in nature, with rhetoricians proclaiming it to be an outside function of the body's movement and voice control. Delivery is merely hand motions, head tilting, voice pitch, foot movement, body position, and nothing more. At the other end of the continuum are theories incorporating a more noetic approach. By *noetic*, I mean having to do with the mind or intellect as opposed to a purely physical process. These rhetoricians believe that when a speech is delivered effectively, the body functions are combined with various intellectual processes. The speaker's thoughts control and are reflected by the physical manifestations of the speaker's body.

Thus, over the centuries and in various cultures, theorists of rhetoric have conceived of delivery as primarily either a physical or noetic activity. This tension between the two ends of the continuum eventually distanced delivery from the other parts of the rhetorical canon and finally led to the split of Cicero's five parts of the successful speech—invention, arrangement, and style remained with written composition, while memory and delivery were delegated to oral composition.

However, as I stated in the introduction, if any parts of the rhetorical canon are ignored or forgotten, then we damage the whole. Therefore, in this chapter, I trace existing theories of delivery through rhetorical history up to the turn of this century in order to understand the tension between the conflicting views of delivery and, ultimately, from this survey to rethink and reformulate a theory of delivery for modern written composition.

CLASSICAL RHETORIC

According to Robert Connors, the people of early Greek times possessed an "oral state of mind," that is, their mode of consciousness was particularly susceptible to oral rhetoric, much more so than people's minds today. Therefore, early Greek orators were able to manipulate Athenian minds, minds that were more readily receptive to any "carefully wrought oral persuasion" ("Greek Rhetoric" 40). This, of course, would have to include the way in which the speech was delivered, but we have little evidence of any sophistic theories on delivery, save descriptions of those sophists rendering their speeches. From these descriptions, we might deduce that the sophists put great store on dramatic eloquence.

One of the first texts that discusses any theory of delivery is Plato's (428–347 BCE) *Cratylus*, in which he stated that a speaker's gestures and voice should be ruled by the needs of the rhetorical situation and by the natural tendency of people to react to imitation as an educational and persuasive strategy. Such physical reaction was essential for the making of meaning (Golden 29). To this end, Plato laid out suggestions for gesture and voice control:

> We should imitate the nature of the thing [subject]; the elevation of our hands to heaven would mean lightness and upwardness; heaviness and downwardness would be expressed by letting them drop to the ground; if we were describing the running of a horse, or any other animal, we should make our bodies and their gestures as like as we could to them....For by bodily imitation only can the body ever express anything....And when we want to express ourselves, either with voice, or tongue, or mouth, the expression is simply their imitation of that which we want to express. (cited in Golden 29)

Later, Plato's student Aristotle (384–322 BCE) downplayed delivery, subordinating it to style. In his *Rhetoric*, Book III, Aristotle viewed delivery as akin to acting, something that he despised. As he wrote, "...delivery is—very properly—not regarded as an elevated subject of inquiry" (165). Nonetheless, he realized that the rhetor must pay attention to the subject, "unworthy as it is," because he cannot afford to ignore it. For him, in fairness, a case should stand alone; nothing should matter beyond the bare facts. However, owing to the "defects of the hearers," the result of a case is considerably affected by other things, such as delivery. In fact, Aristotle believed language used in the speech should actually reflect the points the speaker is trying to make. "The aptness of language is one thing that makes people believe in the truth of your story..." (178). As an example, he stated that to express emotion, the rhetor should employ the language of anger in speaking of outrage. When addressing impiety or foulness, he should use the language of disgust and discreet reluctance to utter a word. The language of exultation should be employed for a tale of glory, and "that of humiliation for a tale of pity..." (178). He instructs the rhetor not to use his voice or countenance in harshness but to allow the words to be harsh. If the rhetor does employ a harsh voice, then "the artificial character of each detail becomes apparent; whereas if you adopt one device and not another, you are using art all the same and yet nobody notices it" (179).

Aristotle surmised that, up to his time, no systematic treatise on the rules of delivery had been composed, so he developed such a treatise. He theorized that delivery should consist of volume of sound, modulation of pitch, and rhythm. Delivery is "a matter of the right management of the voice to express the various emotions" (165). According to the effect needed, the rhetor should speak loudly, softly, or in between, with high, low, or intermediate pitch and with various rhythms to suit various subjects. When these principles of delivery are used appropriately, they produce the same effects as on the theatrical stage (166).

For Aristotle, dramatic ability is a natural gift that cannot be systematically taught. The principles of good diction, however, can be. He theorizes that written, or literary, speeches "owe more of their effect to their diction than to their thought" (166). As an example, he cites the poets who have the human voice at their disposal, the voice being the organ that can "best represent other things." Thus, by systematically categorizing the particular aspects or rules that speakers should follow for a successful speech, Aristotle laid the foundation for future theories about delivery. On the same note, due to his bias against delivery, Aristotle's views also influenced later conceptions of it as undesirable, leading to further tension between theorists of rhetoric.

Following on the heels of Aristotle was Theophrastus (ca. 370–285 BCE), whose greatest influence on rhetorical theory was in the areas of style and delivery (Kennedy, *Persuasion* 273). However, he took delivery in a different direction than his predecessors. According to Athanasius, the philosopher Theophrastus considered delivery to be "the greatest factor an orator has for persuasion" (Kennedy, *Persuasion* 283). Along with elevating the status of delivery in persuasive speaking, Theophrastus gave delivery a more noetic perception. He seemed to believe that physical movement is inspired by the mental act of speaking; he referred "...delivery to first principles and the passions of the soul and the knowledge of these so that the movement of the body and the tone of the voice may be in accordance with the whole science of delivery" (cited in Kennedy, *Persuasion* 283). That is, a speaker must make use of his or her noetic abilities in order to recognize the "passions of the soul" and to be able to use the appropriate motions to reflect those "passions." Knowledge is key for the correct delivery. Thus, Theophrastus established the noetic end of the delivery continuum.

The first major Roman orator who wrote on delivery, Cicero (106–43 BCE), also gave us the five canons of speech. In *De Inventione*, Book I, Cicero defined the five canons of the rhetorical composing process as invention, arrangement, style, memory, and delivery. He stated that delivery is "the control of voice and body in a manner suitable to the dignity of the subject matter and the style" (21). Like Aristotle, Cicero concluded that delivery concerns gesture and voice, but Cicero's theories do not include the more noetic aspects of Theophrastus. In his *Of Oratory*, Cicero wrote that delivery "has the sole and supreme power in oratory; without it, a speaker of the highest mental capacity can be held in no esteem; while one of the moderate abilities, with this qualification, may surpass even those of the highest talent" (255). He believed that each human emotion is accompanied by a unique look, tone, and gesture, and that the whole body, countenance, and voice are moved by affectations of the mind. All the gestures, tones, and looks are "presented to the orator, as colors to the painter, to produce variety" (257). In using these accoutrements, the orator should use full, emphatic force. Cicero continued by giving more explicit instructions to speakers in where, when, and how to use the arms, feet, eyes, and voice.

On the other hand, Cicero also thought, as did Aristotle, that delivery should not enslave the rhetor; he should not "toil like actors at the study of gesture" or become "a slave to his voice, after the manner of Greek tragedians..." ("From *Of Oratory*" 229). However, Cicero did feel that gesture is a great help to the orator and that intonation is the singular and unrivaled recommendation and prop of eloquence.

Cicero classified three kinds of orator, each having a different delivery style. In the *Orator*, he explained that the "Attic" orator, plain and restrained in his language use, will have a rather subdued voice. "His delivery is not that of tragedy nor of the stage; he will employ only slight movements of the body, but will trust a great deal to his expression" (369). The second style of orator, more robust and fuller in voice than the Attic, speaks in a more highly polished style. The third type of orator, who has the greatest power, is "magnificent, opulent, stately and ornate" (375–77). Yet, these orators must beware: if they have the natural ability to be fiery, impetuous and grand, or if they devote energies only to this delivery, then they can be misunderstood or they can lose their audience. If a speaker does not prepare the audience, but simply tries to whip them into a fiery passion without saying anything calmly and mildly, paying no attention to arrangement, precision, clarity or pleasantry, then "he seems to be a raving madman among the sane…" (379). Although Cicero addressed delivery to a greater extent than any other theorist so far, he still had some reservations about delivery, as did Aristotle before him.

By Quintilian's time (35–96 CE), we still see the warning that delivery cannot take the place of attention to language and clarity. He wrote in *Institutes of Oratory* that "unlearned pleaders" try to fain a reputation of speaking well, with energy, through delivery only. "…They bawl on every occasion and bellow out every thing *with uplifted hand*, as they call it, raging like madmen with incessant action, panting and swaggering, and with every kind of gesture and movement of the head" (cited in Bizzell and Herzberg 315). However, all of these outrageous gestures and voicings make a good impression only on an audience of the "lower order." On the other hand, a "polished speaker" can modulate his voice and arrange the parts of his speech effectively and so use delivery adapted to the needs of the speech. He will always keep in mind that modesty is essential in delivery, not the "violence" used by unlearned speakers.

For rhetorical education, Quintilian believed that the best student is the one who can write and speak the best (Smail xxxvi). Therefore, "expression is the main object of instruction" and delivery is a form of that expression. In chapter 11 of Book I, Quintilian described exactly what speech and gesture should consist of: correct voice, hand movement, enunciation, facial expressions, and overall poise. For instance, the student's voice should not be shrill, nor trembling, nor "be imbued with the insolence of a familiar slave" (Smail 60). Letters should be pronounced clearly and sharply. The speaker's lips should not be twisted, nor shall the head be thrown back too far nor bent to either side. The arms should be held straight with the hands at rest, the pose graceful, and the head and eyes must be in harmony with the whole poise of the body. "All men agree that these things belong to the art of delivery, and associate delivery with the orator" (63). He even went so far as to suggest that students should practice dancing as an exercise to learn grace in movement. "For I would not have an orator's gestures as studied as a dancer's movements: all I desire is that something should remain from this youthful training to give us, though we are unconscious of it, that grace of action which learners consciously acquire" (63). Like Aristotle, he feared the artificiality of dramatic performance, but recognized the values of graceful motion.

After Quintilian's time, the Roman Senate lost its power, and dictatorial emperors reigned for three centuries until the fall of the Roman Empire in 410 CE. According to James Murphy, freedom of speech was also lost. This period is termed the *Second Sophistic* by historians, a time of oratorical excesses when attention to subject matter gave way to less controversial matters such as the externals of speech, especially delivery. In the first Sophistic period, eloquence had not been an end unto itself; serious matters, such as the role of truth, the welfare of states, civic issues and so on, took precedence. During the second Sophistic period, with its network of secret police and the unpredictability of the Roman leaders, Murphy argues that no orator felt safe delivering a deliberative or political speech (*Synoptic History* 177–78). Then, it is no wonder that Eunapius, in *Lives of the Sophists*, regaled us with the details of Prohaeresius's vehement delivery but did not report the subject on which he spoke. Clearly, the sophists of that period were interested in the way a thing was said, not in what was said (Murphy, *Middle Ages* 37–38). Thus, delivery took on those flourishes that the early Greeks had despised. Orators became more like actors with their grand fiery emotions, prancing about before the audience. Language, even truth and substance itself, had lost out in favor of physicality, Aristotle's worst nightmare. However, delivery soon took on negative connotations, and eventually, procedures in court barred full-scale opening addresses or summations like those of the previous era. Thus, by the end of the Roman Empire, we see a decline in interest in delivery (Kennedy, *Classical Rhetoric* 105), and a greater emphasis placed on the other elements of Cicero's theory—invention, arrangement, style, and memory—causing delivery to suffer a distancing from the rhetorical canon.

MEDIEVAL AND RENAISSANCE RHETORIC

The concepts of Cicero survived this onslaught on rhetoric and continued through the Middle Ages as the guiding light of rhetoricians. (Examples of rhetoricians who used Cicero's concepts as their foundations include Boethius, 480–524; Robert of Basevorn, fl. 1322; and George of Trebizond, 1395–1472). In fact, Ciceronian rhetoric also became the basis for English rhetoric. Alcuin (ca. 781), who established an education system in France for Charlemagne, was the first Englishman to compose a work (written in Latin) specifically outlining Cicero's five canons. Alcuin spent little time discussing the values of delivery, but the most important aspect is that Cicero's influence had now crossed the ocean and would be the basis of the rhetoric of such writers as Geoffrey of Vinsauf (ca. 1208), John of Garland (1195–1272), Gervase of Melkley (ca. 1210), Matthew of Vendome (ca. 1175), and Thomas Waleys (ca. 1349). All of these theorists treated delivery very briefly. Like their contemporary Alexander of Ashby (ca. 1210), they believed "delivery should not be proud nor rough nor unctuous nor harsh, but modest and humble, agreeable, and consistent with the plan of the sermon and the nature of the subject matter" (Murphy, *Middle Ages* 313–14).

As the aforementioned term *sermon* may indicate, the majority of rhetoricians in the Middle Ages were also ministers. The particular rhetorical situations they faced may explain why each of them treated delivery so perfunctorily. (Possibly, they believed they were speaking to a captive audience and did not need to bother keeping the audience's attention or engaging them in the speech. Perhaps, the ministers thought the audience would pay attention merely because the threat of hell and damnation was so intimidating.) In *De arte praedicatoria* (ca. 1199), Alain de Lille, a Cistercian monk, laid the foundation of preaching with a more rhetorical approach to pulpit eloquence than had previously been followed, but he made little use of classical rhetorical theory in organizing his treatise. Here, delivery is addressed only as a caution against display (cited in Bizzell and Herzberg 378). Therefore, all other rhetoricians of the time, particularly those connected with the church, may have taken their lead from Alcuin and tried to guard against any showy display in the pulpit by limiting their discussion of delivery. Nevertheless, by the late 1600s, pulpit oratory became the target of frequent attacks over stylistic excesses. Thus, church-related rhetoricians, such as Fenelon (who will be discussed later), called for the need of natural delivery and gesture as opposed to artificial, contrived movements.

It was not until 1509 that the first treatise on rhetoric was printed. Stephen Hawes published *Pastime of Pleasure*, an allegory of learning written as a poem in which Lady "Rethoryke" instructs the poet La Graunde Amoure in her art. Of delivery, or "pronuncyacyon," the lady states that the standards of delivery both for the speaker and the reader are formulated by considering the audience. For instance, a sophisticated audience requires that the speaker be cultivated and refined. Her instructions to poets telling their tales are to avoid rudeness and to be gentle and seemly because the purpose of their speech is to refine manners and remove folly (Howell, *Logic* 84).

Erasmus, through his study of Agricola, had transferred invention and arrangement from rhetoric to logic and limited rhetoric to merely style and delivery (Kennedy, *Classical Rhetoric* 206). Agricola also had a great impact on another rhetorician, who would in turn impact rhetoric for centuries to come, the Frenchman Peter Ramus(1515–1572). Ramus, too, relegated rhetoric to the study of style and delivery, each of which he also divided: style into tropes and figures, and delivery into voice and gesture. These concepts were not new; Quintilian had addressed them in his *Institutio*, but now delivery was separated from any content. Rhetoric was now empty, left only with the names, derivations, and literary applications of tropes and figures, along with commands to issue on voice and gesture (Howell, *Eighteenth Century* 78). Here, we see delivery return to the purely physical end of the continuum, completely divorced from any intellectual processes. Subsequently, this divorce led to greater tensions between the conflicting views of delivery, the physical and noetic, as Ramus's influence traveled across several continents.

In 1574, Ramus's concepts were introduced to England by Roland MacIlmaine, the first Briton to translate Ramus's theories into English. At this point, Ramistic rhetoric eclipsed Ciceronian as a whole canon in England for half a century (Howell, "English Backgrounds" 31). Ramus also infiltrated the United States shortly thereafter by way of a text written by Omer Talon (also known as Audomarus Talaeus). His *Rhetorica*, among those texts used to teach rhetoric at Harvard, had great circulation in the colonies (Howell, "English Backgrounds" 49).

In 1544, Talon published *Institutiones Oratoriae*, later known as *Rhetorica*. His theories and definitions so closely followed Ramus's that many critics thought that Talon was Ramus's pseudonym. At the same time, Talon took Ramus one step further, widening the gap between physical and noetic theories of delivery. His rhetoric became totally rule governed; his discussion of delivery centered on which rules must be followed in what situation. In effect, Talon told the orator that the delivery will be right if the rule is followed, not that the response will be appropriate if the situation exists so as to make that response truly reflect the speaker's pattern of thought and feeling (Howell, *Fenelon* 21). Thus, Talon made delivery even more empty and ingenious, no longer concerned with audience and context.

In response to the tendencies of such a popular doctrine, Francis Bacon (1561–1626) took delivery (and rhetoric in general) in a different direction. Bacon studiously kept the ancient terms of Ciceronian rhetoric but chose to incorporate those terms into his own philosophy. For this effort, in his *Advancement of Learning*, he reduced the five canons to the four "Arts Intellectual":

...for man's labour is to *invent* that which is *sought* or *propounded*; or to *judge* that which is invented; to *retain* that which is *judged*; or to *deliver over* that which is *retained*. So as the arts must be four; Art of Inquiry or Invention; Art of Examination or Judgement; Art of Custody or Memory; and Art of Elocution or Tradition. (cited in Bizzell and Herzberg 625–26)

For Bacon, style and delivery were conflated as the single term *tradition*, which he defined as "the means by which knowledge is used and incorporated into social institutions, which are maintained in memory" (624). Thus, the function of tradition went beyond mere style and delivery in a persuasive speech to the whole enterprise of transferring or expressing the speaker's knowledge to the audience in speech, in writing, in exposition, or in controversy (Howell, *Logic* 369). In other words, Bacon's reinterpretation of delivery as elocution or tradition, along with his idea of rhetoric as the "illustration of tradition," restored to rhetoric its original communicative function, the task of reaching and persuading humans, a task that had been divorced from rhetoric by Ramus. Through Bacon, delivery moved from an empty, rule-governed, merely physical device back to a noetic process that engaged the audience with the orator's speech.

Bacon divided tradition into organ, method, and illustration. Organ is either speech or writing, as he quoted from Aristotle: "Words are the images of cogitations, and letters are the images of words" (cited in Bizzell and Herzberg 628). However, Bacon believed that words are not the only means of serious thinking; other senses can also express thought. For instance, in primitive societies, or for those who are deaf mutes, we see "that men's minds are expressed in gestures...because the characters are accepted more generally than the languages do extend..." (628).

Regarding method, Bacon wrote:

For as knowledges are now delivered, there is a kind of contract of error between the deliverer and the receiver: for he that delivereth knowledge desireth to deliver it in such form as may be best believed, and not as may be best examined; and he that receiveth knowledge desireth rather present satisfaction than expectant inquiry; and so rather not to doubt than not to err: glory making the author not to lay open his weakness, and sloth making the disciple not to know his strength. (cited in Howell, *Logic* 370)

Bacon believed that both the speaker and hearer have different expectations from the delivery of a speech. The deliverer wants the knowledge to be believed, and the hearer wants not to work hard at understanding the knowledge being delivered. Yet, both these participants in the speech act must use their intellectual processes, the speaker to deliver the speech and the hearer to understand it.

The third part of Bacon's tradition, illustration, was the "shedding of light so as to make anything visible to the eyes. In other words, illustration within the context of theory of communication would mean the shedding of light so as to make knowledge visible and hence deliverable to an audience" (Howell, *Logic* 371). That is, Bacon wanted the speaker to make the topic clear and visible to an audience, through physical gesture and vocal display if necessary, so that they could see it with their eyes, rather than merely hear it through the words. The more ways in which a speaker can engage an audience, the better his or her chances are to make the audience understand the points being made.

Even though Bacon did at times mention the physical actions that were to accompany delivery, he still contended that gesture and counte- nance were mirrors of the mind, as he wrote in a piece to Queen Elizabeth I:

> For the lineaments of the body disclose the dispositions and inclinimations of the end in general; but the motions and gestures of the countenance and parts do not only so, but disclose likewise the season of access, and the present humour and state of the mind and will. For as your Majesty says most aptly and elegantly, "As the tongue speaketh to the ear so the gesture speaketh to the eye." (*On Communication* 166)

Thus, we can see that Bacon's delivery, besides incorporating some physical activity, also took on a more noetic cast, close to that of Theophrastus. Theophrastus believed the "passions of the soul" and the knowledge of them moved the speaker to physical gestures; Bacon saw delivery as the physical display of the "present state of the mind and will."

Another theorist who sided against Ramistic rhetoric was French Arch- bishop Francois Fenelon (1651–1715). He, too, like Theophrastus and Bacon, considered delivery to be an outward and visible sign of an inner state of conviction and feeling:

> The manner of saying things makes visible the manner in which one feels them, and it is this which strikes the listeners the more....The movement of the body is then a painting of the thoughts of the soul....And that painting ought to be a genuine likeness. It is necessary that everything in it represent vividly and naturally the sentiments of him who is speaking and the nature of the things he speaks of. (Howell, *Fenelon* 97, 99)

He enumerated some guidelines, though, about the physical movement of the orator. He claimed that it is unnecessary for the orator to be forever moving the arms while speaking, that the eyes are the most important feature ("A single glance thrown to good purpose will strike to the depths of the heart"), and that the same intensity of action accompanies the same intensity of voice (Howell, *Fenelon* 97, 103, 105). Throughout his theories ran the theme of the intellectual connections to delivery. Thus, we may place Fenelon closer to the noetic end of the delivery continuum, combining the physical and intellectual.

Through the Medieval and Renaissance periods, we see the increased movement of delivery back and forth on the continuum between the purely physical and the noetic theories. During the Renaissance, Ramus and Bacon seemed to galvanize the division of the theories and, subsequently, heightened the tension between the two sides. As we shall see next, the rise of purely physical theories of delivery increased this tension and heralded the distancing of delivery from Cicero's original rhetorical canon.

THE ELOCUTIONARY MOVEMENT

Like those rhetoricians before them, the elocutionists and their detractors can also be divided into those who professed delivery from a Ciceronian aspect (the purely physical elements) and those who sided with Theophrastus and Bacon (the more noetic elements). Due to the nature of the movement, the majority of the elocutionists were Ciceronians because elocution called for even more rigid rules governing gesture and voice than had been proposed in previous rhetorical theory, a stance that eventually leads to the further distancing of delivery from the canon of rhetoric. An example is the forerunner of the Elocutionary Movement, John Ward, who was appointed professor of rhetoric at Gresham College, England, in 1720.

To begin, Ward insisted that the art of elocution should never be separated from the other rhetorical canons: "rhetoric is an integral whole in respect to the four parts that comprise it, namely, invention, disposition, elocution, and pronunciation" (cited in Howell, *Eighteenth Century* 113). But Ward harkened back to the Ciceronian definition of delivery as gesture and voice, to which he dedicates a chapter each in *A System of Oratory* (1759). In his text, he advised that "The motions of the body should rise therefore in proportion to the vehemence, and energy of the expression, as the natural and genuine effect of it" or "It [the body] should not long continue in the same position, but be constantly changing, though the motion be very moderate" (329–30). He continued with rather elaborate advice on how to manage the head, eyes, arms, hands, chest, feet, and so on. His entire treatment of delivery may be summed up in one of his passages: "What fits well upon one, will appear very awkward in another. Everyone, therefore, should first endeavor to know himself, and manage accordingly" (376).

If Ward was a forerunner of the movement, Michel Le Faucheur actually set the stage with his Ciceronian approach to delivery. In 1727, an English translation of the work of Le Faucheur (late 1500s–1657), a French Protestant clergyman, was published. According to Howell, La Faucheur wrote one of the most respectable works of scholarship during the whole of the elocutionary movement, a work that became one of the leading treatises on delivery and heralded Sheridan's theories of elocution (*Eighteenth Century* 168–69). For instance, La Faucheur's advice to clergy and to lawyers invoked purely physical delivery: "there is nothing like a fine way of *Speaking* and *Gesture* to make them take notice of a *Plea*....The best *Cause* in the world may soon be lost for want of *Action*" (cited in Howell, *Eighteenth Century* 174). That "action" consisted of voice and gesture, gesture including the whole body, head, face, eyes, eyebrows, mouth, lips, shoulders, arms, legs, and so on. In La Faucheur's opinion, the most important movements were made by the hands and eyes.

La Faucheur's view of the oratorical art later became an obsession with elocutionists. He believed that to become a great rhetor, one had to simply acquire the air, gallantry, and grace of good pronunciation and gesture. Not only would the person achieve the eloquence of the ancient Greek and Roman masters but also the greatness of character and eloquence of speech in the eighteenth century. To La Faucheur's followers, delivery was all that mattered in oratory; excellence in delivery could make up for all deficiencies in invention, arrangement and style, whereas the opposite was not true. However, in the original text, La Faucheur himself believed that delivery could not be the sole member of the art; rhetoric involved more than just delivery. According to Howell, Le Faucheur's English translator, in his own preface, La Faucheur constantly leaned toward making delivery the main end and design of rhetoric, an attitude that was passed on to English elocutionists, particularly Sheridan. Thus, La Faucheur's position on delivery, at the purely physical end of the continuum, added fuel to the growing elocutionary movement.

Between 1730 and 1785, the first works devoted solely to delivery, both in England and America, began to appear. John Mason, one of the first authors to concentrate on delivery, in 1748 gave to this new separate discipline the name of *elocution* and within a few short years, the term came to mean *delivery* rather than its Latin definition *style* (Guthrie, "Rhetorical Theory" 48–49). Following this lead by Mason, in 1762, Thomas Sheridan published his *Course of Lectures on Elocution*. In fact, Sheridan gave up a career as an actor to devote himself to elocution and correcting language. To him, the only part of ancient rhetoric that was of any importance was delivery (Kennedy, *Classical Rhetoric* 228). Although he utilized Quintilian's words about delivery, he used them as though Quintilian suggested that only delivery presents difficulties to the student of eloquence. Although Quintilian only tackled delivery after an exhaustive treatment of the other four canons, Sheridan wrote as if true excellence in oratory lay solely in mastering delivery (Howell, *Eighteenth Century* 233).

Sheridan's advice to the orator was to be natural and to treat public speaking as a form of conversation. The orator's gestures, likewise, are to be natural, meaning "not mechanical," rather "springing from human nature" ("A Course" 729). His definition of elocution was "the just and graceful management of the voice, countenance, and gesture in speaking" (Sheridan, *Course* 38). He also believed that we need more than mere language to communicate:

> But as there are other things which pass in the mind of man, beside ideas; as he is not wholly made up of intellect, but on the contrary, the passions, and the fancy, compose great part of his complicated frame; as the operations of these are attended with an infinite variety of emotions in the mind, both in kind and degree; it is clear, that unless there be some means found, of manifesting those emotions, all that passes in the mind of one man cannot be communicated to another. Now, as in order to know what another knows, and in the same manner that he knows it, an exact transcript of the ideas which pass in the mind of one man, must be made by sensible marks, in the mind of another; so in order to feel what another feels, the emotions which are in the mind of one man, must also be communicated to that of another, by sensible marks. (99)

Those sensible marks for Sheridan were "tones, looks, and gestures" (100). Through this stumbling around about people's minds, Sheridan seemed to take a more noetic stance on the continuum, although later his ideas and theories were bastardized into a more purely physical and mechanical delivery, something he would hardly call recognizably his own theory.

Gilbert Austin ushered British elocutionists into the nineteenth century with his *Chironomia; or a Treatise on Rhetorical Delivery* (1806). Unlike Sheridan, Austin distrusted the natural method of delivery. Therefore, he devised his own detailed choreographed system of speech performances that he believed was flexible enough not to dictate to an orator, but merely suggest. "It is a language, which may be used to express every variety of opinion" (Sheridan, "A Course" 739). His symbols included instructions for loudness and tone of voice, for speed of speaking, for movement of head, hands, body, and feet. A text with his marking system resembles a piece of music to be performed. Austin diligently examined ancient Greek and Roman rhetoricians and kept his readers constantly aware of the background of delivery. In this, his text was far superior to Sheridan, who had little knowledge of classical rhetoric, but Austin's Ciceronian-style elocution rendered rhetoric narrow and sterile (Howell, *Eighteenth Century* 251–52). With him, delivery became a rule-governed set of motions to be memorized and used by the orator at the appropriate time, a type of dance step. He treated the externals of oratory, as did many other elocutionists, having no concern for the noetic factor in determining how people express themselves.

One other achievement we can recognize Austin for is the first use of the word "delivery": "The term elocution is, by this acceptation, diverted from its original signification as established by the ancient rhetoricians.... To express what the Roman writers understood by *pronunciatio* and *actio*, we shall use the word Delivery, which is already established, in this sense, in our language" (2–3). Thus, Austin initiated the terminology we continue to use today.

Another treatise that was influential in nineteenth-century England and America was James Rush's *The Philosophy of the Human Voice* (1827). Here, he described in detail, pitch, timbre, glides, and all sounds that a human voice should use in oratory (Stewart 137–39). He attempted to give elocution a scientific basis through the use of psychological data and the examination of the anatomy of the voice mechanism. His concern was not to give a set of rhetorical rules but to give a physiological foundation to speech. Therefore, I would have to classify Rush's theories as purely physical because of his concern for the externals of delivery. Austin and Rush both greatly influenced American elocutionists who shared an interest in how the expressive use of voice and gesture enhances emotional appeals and clarity of understanding (N. Johnson 155).

The continental elocutionary movement also led to the rise of the Delsarte System of Expression in the United States. Francois Delsarte, a French teacher of vocal music and operatic acting in Paris from 1839 to 1871, never published his theories in any form. Even so, several people who had spent some time training with him purported to know the "true" Delsartian methods and published many books and magazine articles in the

United States. Despite its popularity, no adequate formulation of Delsartian principles and practices was ever made and thus, the system was in perennial dispute (Wallace, *History* 204).

Karl Wallace describes Delsarte's system as a "psuedo-philosophy, claiming to be a science, which organized all arts and sciences according to a plan which was based, in essence, on orthodox Catholic doctrine" (*History* 204). He states that life, mind, and soul are expressed by certain agents; that is, the vocal expresses life, words express mind, and movement expresses soul. The concept of movement expressing soul possibly accounts for the emphasis that American Delsartians put upon gesture and pantomime. Wallace concludes that it is unlikely Delsarte placed any more emphasis on physical aspects of his system than on vocal. Regardless, in America, the Delsartian system became, in essence, a system of physical culture, a routine mechanical form for teaching expression of emotion largely through gesture and body position, accompanied by statue posing, tableaux, and so on (205, 216). Statue posing and tableaux consisted of posing without speaking, to represent abstract concepts and/or emotions, pictures, or scenes.

In the late 1800s, the American market was flooded with publications on the so-called Delsartian system, many of them written by women. I surmise that because much of the Delsarte system was used as parlor entertainment, women were permitted to take part in such nonpublic speaking. Seeing the system also as a psuedoeducational practice, the women would be even more intrigued during a time when they were not generally accepted into higher education. Two Delsartian manuals were written by Genevieve Stebbins. In 1902, she composed the *Delsarte System of Expression* in which she stated:

> To place ourselves en rapport with the idea or thing, to create a living image of it in the mind and reproduce it with the vividness of its own natural life, is the quintessence of all that Delsarte or any other man can formulate in the art of expression.... [T]he spirit of Delsarte's idea...was a perfect union of mind, body and soul. In other words, a union of spontaneous emotion with artistic expression (389, 442).

If Stebbins was correct in her statements, then Delsarte seemed to side with the more noetic stance of delivery, that is, it expresses a concern for a union of mind and body. In fact, that may have been what Delsarte himself originally had in mind. On the contrary, with its concentration on posing and tableaux, the reality is more that the Delsarte method in practice is more of a culmination of the physical end of the continuum. The physical/aesthetic entirely obviates the need for discourse or the need for the intellect.

In the eighteenth and nineteenth centuries, with the strong influence of the purely physical, elocution achieved new heights of rule-governed delivery. More and more, theorists invoked rigid rules, moving further away from the noetic end of the continuum, until the Delsarte system altogether replaced the need for discourse. At this point, delivery had finally been totally removed from the rhetorical canon.

NEOCLASSICAL RHETORIC

In the midst of the elocutionary movement, George Campbell, Hugh Blair, and Richard Whately added another dimension to the division of delivery theory. Campbell, a Scottish professor of divinity, Blair, a Scottish professor of rhetoric, and Whately, a British doctor of divinity, all followed the romanticists, denying rules and regulations and calling for a "natural manner" of delivery, one that would trust in the orator's own thought–emotion for guidance. Although they denounced the purely physical elements that the elocutionary movement had idealized, they did find a legitimate place for delivery, albeit a redefined natural physical delivery.

According to Wallace, two points of view underlie their concept: the speaker should concentrate on the subject, and, freed from rigid rules, should remain confident in the effectiveness of delivery that springs spontaneously from heartfelt attempts at communication (*History* 97).

Campbell, Blair, and Whately all listed three forms of delivery: speaking extemporaneously, speaking from memory, and reading. Campbell and Whately agreed that extempore is the best method (Wallace, *History* 100). Yet, all three rhetoricians had their own concepts about delivery. Campbell divided delivery into two parts: grammatical pronunciation, distinct articulation of vowels and consonants with the appropriate syllabic emphasis; and rhetorical pronunciation, giving voice to sentences that reveal the feeling of truth and justness of the thought conveyed by them and placing emphasis on the proper word of the sentence. He placed gesture under this second heading, but he had little to say on the subject (98, 100). Campbell dwelled mostly on the vocal aspects of delivery, pronunciation, but believed in a "natural" physical delivery, not one governed by rigid rules.

For his part, in his *Lectures on Rhetoric and Belles Lettres* (1783), Blair defined delivery as "the management of the voice and gesture" (N. Johnson 44), but he also claimed that speaking effectively in public did not come from following rigid rules for voice and gesture. Instead, a speaker is to be earnest and speak from the heart (Howell, *Eighteenth Century* 664). Like Austin and Rush, Blair's major interest was in delivery practices that increase the impression that ideas and emotions have on others. In contrast, however, he believed that the natural method was far more conducive to engaging the passions and imagination rather than to applying indiscriminately gestures and actions learned by rote:

> The capital direction, which ought never to be forgotten, is to copy the proper tones for expressing every sentiment from those which Nature dictates to us, in conversation with others; to speak always with her voice; and not to form to ourselves a fantastic public manner, from an absurd fancy of its being more beautiful than a natural one" (cited in N. Johnson 44).

In her study of nineteenth-century rhetoric, Nan Johnson finds that "A pervasive interest in the organic principles of human nature" influences Blair's concept of delivery that renders "words fully significant by embodying natural sentiments in tones and gestures" (49). Hence, Blair's concept of delivery seems to fall at the more noetic end of the continuum more so than Campbell.

Blair also diverged from the elocutionists by refusing to use the term elocution, which he thought was the proper word for style, whereas pronunciation was the correct word for delivery. By being traditional with his word choice, Blair also heralded the modern era of new rhetoric that did not subscribe to the terminology nor the rhetorical theory of the elocutionists (Howell, *Eighteenth Century* 665).

Following Blair was Richard Whately with his *Elements of Rhetoric* (1828). He too expounded on the natural manner, which was what "one naturally falls into who is *really speaking*, in earnest, and with a mind *exclusively* intent on what he has to say" (236). He believed there are three qualities of delivery: *perspicuity*, making the meaning fully understandable to the audience; *energy*, conveying meaning forcibly; and *elegance*, conveying meaning agreeably. Again, though, he fell back on nature, stating that the elements of these three qualities will be suggested spontaneously to the speaker naturally. Nevertheless, Whately refused to discuss any physical action, saying that the rigid rules of the elocutionary movement had disgusted orators so much that speakers were now in the habit of standing totally still when speaking (Wallace, *History* 99). Because he advocated having the "mind exclusively intent" during delivery and refused to mention the physical aspects, I am led to believe that Whately fell closer to the noetic end of the continuum than many of the other elocutionists of the time. Thus, Campbell, Blair, and Whately maintained the bias against physical delivery, even perhaps strengthening it, and thereby helped perpetuate the tension and bias among the various theoretical opponents.

At this time in America, Campbell, Blair, and Whately, plus many classical rhetoricians, had their impact on John Quincy Adams, the first Boylston Professor of Rhetoric and Oratory at Harvard (1805). In fact, his theories of rhetoric were an attempt to break from the English rhetorics that had taken elocution to a new high, although the popularity of elocution kept the classics in the background.

Adams, in his definition of delivery, returned to the classical terms *pronunciatio* and *actio*, which he combines to mean delivery. He berated his contemporaries who had usurped *elocutio* to describe gesticulation and states that it would be ludicrous if the classical orators had merely meant bodily motion (171–73). Adams' rhetorical theories, like some other American rhetoricians, were a restatement of classical rhetoric; his theories followed more the Ciceronian model, that of focusing on the physical only. In his lectures, he advised a slow rate of speech, a variety of tone, and sufficient volume to reach all the audience. He also briefly summarized Quintilian's suggestions for gesture, but Adams gave no instructions for training the voice; in fact, oral practice was barely mentioned. An interesting aside: Adams' theory of delivery, according to reports, was not indicative of his own practice as a public speaker. He himself spoke quickly and at times softly. Friends even described his manner of delivery as cold and lacking in charisma (Rahskopf 441).

Although a successor to Adams in the Boylston chair, Edward Channing did not espouse the same Ciceronian ideas of delivery. Rather, like Bacon, Channing believed treatments of delivery should be primarily a matter of giving "nature free room for making her spontaneous suggestions" and "by making ...natural and necessary experiments upon her power" (cited in N. Johnson 75). That is, instead of adhering to rigid rules that stifle natural motions in accordance with speaking, Channing thought for delivery an orator should call on his or her own instincts and intellect when speaking. To Channing, delivery should be inspired by noetic processes, not artificial rules.

THE RISE OF COMPOSITION
IN THE UNITED STATES

By the middle of the nineteenth century, the elocutionary movement began to meet with antagonism in academia. It had become too much a performer's art and no longer met the needs of the students being trained in written literacy for professions in law and ministry (Wallace, *History* 189). According to Albert Kitzhaber, the issues raised by the American Revolutionary

War led to a greater emphasis on oratory and debate in academia. The severity of those issues and the possible outcomes forced people into discussions of the future and how to resolve the problems they faced as a new nation. However, elocution's simultaneous growing popularity increasingly narrowed oratorical training to one aspect, delivery, driving it further and further from the rest of the rhetorical canon: "During the first half of the nineteenth century oral rhetoric came to be identified even more closely with elocution, which usually had its own texts and professors" (31). For instance, one rhetorician, Ebenezer Porter, further divorced delivery from the rhetorical canon by defining it alone as communication in and of itself: " Delivery, in the most general sense, is the communication of our thoughts to others, by oral language.... [I]t is the chief instrument by which one mind acts on others..." (cited in N. Johnson 149–50). Possibly due to theories such as these, formal rhetoric was studied as a body of knowledge worth knowing for its own sake, without any practical application to speaking or writing (Kitzhaber 32).

All the same, with the rise of enrollments and lack of teachers, written composition began to take the place of training in rhetoric. By 1860, delivery came to be considered apart from rhetoric and was taught as a separate subject at Harvard (Anderson 86). Soon rhetorical theorists also began to concentrate on written discourse, regarding elocution as an ancillary art. Because they believed delivery related only to oral presentation and not to the laws of written discourse, most rhetoricians refused to include it in their analyses of rhetorical principles. For instance, David J. Hill stated:

> Elocution has long been regarded as a part of Rhetoric, but it is by itself too important and extensive a subject to be treated as a division of rhetorical science. It does, indeed contribute to render spoken discourse more effective, but so does elegant chirography or clear typography improve the effectiveness of written thought. Rhetoric treats of discourse in general, not of written or spoken discourse in particular. (5)

Thus, Hill divided elocution–delivery from rhetoric and claimed that delivery is only useful when adapting knowledge to oral expression. Although most rhetoricians at this time did not include delivery in the canons of rhetoric, many of them did acknowledge the importance of delivery to the public speaker. Like Hill, these rhetoricians equated delivery to elocution, not seeing delivery in any broader view. Because they were teaching written composition, they did not consider delivery to be in their domain.

Henry N. Day agreed with Hill that elocution and vocal delivery should be separated into different categories. He stated that the art of rhetoric could not be considered complete until the ideas to be communicated are actually conveyed to the mind of the audience. Therefore, rhetoric must employ delivery, but the mode of communication is not essential. The thought may be conveyed through speech or writing. Accordingly, elocution is not a necessary part of rhetoric: "We do have a complete product of art when the thought is embodied in a proper form of language" (cited in Bizzell and Herzberg 870). Therefore, further exertion of artistic power is not necessary in order to give the thought expression. No oratorical dexterity, no skill to speak, is needed to write: "We have then the limits of a complete art before elocution" (870).

In addition, he stated that elocution and the art of rhetoric are so distinct that one person can have a great proficiency in one or the other but not necessarily in both. Also, the modes of training in their different arts is quite different; therefore, they should be separate for the convenience of the teacher and student.

Nevertheless, Day was not above writing a text for training in elocution. In his *The Art of Elocution* (1859), Day set down quite plainly a method of vocal training in the introduction: "In training the voice, there are three things which need to be distinctly regarded. They are, the first, acquisition of a ready command over the respective organs employed in speech; secondly, the increase of the strength of the organs; and thirdly, the promotion of flexibility in the organs" (cited in Robb 116). He continued with minute details on how to use the voice correctly in delivery, especially using the four functions of speech: pitch, quality, time, and force, which are a means of expressing thought and feeling. Most of all, though, Day explained that the mode of delivery should be determined by the occasion and by the character of the material:

> The occasion on which the piece is to be delivered, will determine the loudness and abruptness of the utterance, or the degree of force, and also, to some extent, the melody and quantity....The *character of the piece* will affect the determination in regard to all the various functions of the voice to be employed. The kind and degree of passion should be ascertained first. This will generally determine the melody to be adopted....The *thought* should then be carefully analyzed, in order to determine, first, the relative prominence of the ideas to be expressed; and secondly, the relations between the different phrases. Finally, the structure of the pieces as to verbal expression should be studied, in order to determine the emphatic words, whether emphatic on their own account, or as representatives for a phrase; and, also, the degree of prominence to be given them. (cited in Robb 118)

Although Day believed that elocution was a separate entity from rhetoric, on the topic of delivery, he still aligns himself with the purely physical theorists by emphasizing the voice and expression that are to be used in delivery.

Likewise, Alexander Melville Bell, in *Principles of Elocution* (1878), followed the purely physical model of delivery, focusing primarily on naming and illustrating techniques. One set of rules Bell covered is the properties of the voice: articulation, inflection, accent, emphasis, pause, force, time, and pitch. He gave detailed analyses for each of the properties as he did for guidelines of action and gesture (N. Johnson 151–55).

The absence from a textbook or treatise of a discussion of elocution or delivery is just as telling as is its inclusion. John Franklin Genung, in *Practical Elements of Rhetoric*, omitted any consideration of delivery, probably because of his conception of rhetoric as a literary art, an art of composition (including the writing of speeches), and because of the inclusion of separate courses in elocution in the college curriculum (Allen 239). For Genung and his contemporaries, "rhetoric was not concerned with the method of delivery, whether written or oral, only with the content and its verbal expression. Elocution was as foreign to rhetoric as penmanship" (Ettlich 285). From an institutional perspective, one possible reason for this divorcing of elocution from rhetoric may have been the ever-increasing divisiveness of the college curriculum, as mentioned previously. Professors and departments were laying claim to their own "turf," and because elocution was taught in other areas (for instance, theater arts), it was not acceptable to have an overlap of the course in other departments. Another reason for the separation of delivery from rhetoric could be that Genung did not acknowledge that delivery could be anything other than physical; he did not consider the possible noetic properties of delivery.

Although neglected by many academicians, delivery (and elocution) did not die. In 1888, Samuel Silas Curry organized the School of Expression, whose study and practice is based in psychology. Opposed to popular theories, he believed "that elocution should be primarily a training of the mind and the development of an ability to think creatively" (Wallace, *History* 194). According to Curry, "Expression implies cause, means and effect. It is a natural effect of a natural cause, and hence is governed by all the laws of nature's processes. The cause is in the mind, the means are the voice and the body" (cited in Wallace, *History* 196). Curry thought that humans must function as unified wholes; thus, it is impossible to detach outward expression from noetic analysis of the material to be delivered. In a three-way interaction between mind, voice, and body, voice and body could not be left to flounder "but...developed into a flexible mechanism which will adequately express the mind or soul of the speaker" (cited in Wallace, *History* 197). Although he advocated training the mind over training the voice and body, he thought of the three as a whole, and the time devoted to physical exercises is always considered only as "practice to enable the speaker to respond naturally and normally to noetic stimulation" (cited in Wallace, *History* 197).

In a similar vein, Edward N. Kirby's *Public Speaking and Reading* (1896) proposed an elocutionary method that could be used for the public reading of poetry and for rhetorical speaking, a method that emphasized a noetic aspect of delivery. Kirby stated that his theory of public speaking demands a certain creative ability and is based on conversational speech. As he described it, the main problem for the student is to secure the right noetic action to which the body would respond. He insisted that the body and mind work together:

> For the solution of this Main Problem, both the subjective and the objective treatment are employed. The subjective treatment deals directly with the content of the mind; that is, with the thought and feeling.
>
> The thought and feeling are analyzed and dwelt upon. Related ideas are brought forward; and thus, by dealing with the factors of the mind directly, we seek to promote right mental action with reference to the subject-matter and its expression....
>
> In the objective treatment, however, we call attention to the agents (the chest, the mouth, the hands, etc.), and to the elements (emphasis, pitch, etc.), expressive of the thought and feeling.
>
> The objective treatment is based upon the fact that bodily states affect mental states; hence, by assuming the physical attitude, the corresponding mental state is initiated and promoted. We not only entreat the angry man not to be angry, but also coax him to sit down and not speak so loudly.... This treatment, reaching the mind by calling attention to the physical states, is the shorthand method of everyday life. (cited in Robb 182)

Thus, Kirby attempted to scientize the field by coming up with an objective approach that justifies why delivery is so important. Of course, during this time period, the scientific model impacted all disciplines. And rhetoric did not escape the influence. Kirby used this scientific language to agree with many of the theorists before him—that delivery should be viewed as noetic.

Elocution, though, was in such disrepute in academia by the end of the century that oral rhetoric usually did not appear in any books published between 1893 and 1900 (Kitzhaber 86). Such disdain for elocution may have stemmed from movements like Delsarte's that put such an emphasis on physical posturing, not on content. Academics may have seen this as cheap and too degrading for intellectual pursuits, reflecting Aristotle's bias against acting. The elocution that did remain was being challenged by new courses in public-speaking broader than merely voice and gesture. The courses included great emphasis on content and audience appeal. A few courses even incorporated topical issues for debates. For instance, in her public-speaking classes (as well as composition classes) Gertrude Buck, rhetoric professor at Vassar (1897–1922), used such topics as "Speculation is detrimental to the interests of the community," "The Inter-State Commerce law should be repealed," and "The public should own and control the telephone service" (Buck 168).

Meanwhile, the daily theme became a fixture in schools during this time, but due to overwhelming masses of student writing, a few professors by 1900 were urging the importance of oral composition, rather than only written composition. This was seen as a practical solution to the mountains of daily themes, yet it still gave some training in composition. However, the rhetoricians also tried to give sound reasons why teachers needed to return to oral work in composition, an attempt to rejoin delivery to the other elements of the rhetorical canon. For instance, Fred Newton Scott and John Villiers Denney protested the "isolation of written from spoken discourse." They claimed "the artificial separation of two things which naturally belong together takes the heart out of both of them" (cited in Kitzhaber 86).

Denney alone made an important contribution to the reshaping of speech. He introduced the term *oral English* in order to include speech instruction in his department at The Ohio State University. He believed that the art of public speech had become less of a profession and more a requirement of many. Thus, delivery needed to have less emphasis on gesture and voice and needed to be more thought-centered (Faules 106). With this view, Denney seemed to follow the noetic view of delivery.

Nonetheless, during this period, the late nineteenth and the early twentieth century, the separation of oral and written communication became so divisive that writing evolved into a medium through which to convey experience and information silently. According to Michael Halloran, "the voice of the orator was not supposed to be present in the dailies [Barrett] Wendell's students wrote for class or in the business letters and professional reports they would write in post-collegiate life" (Murphy, *Short History* 172–73). Thus, invention, arrangement, and style became associated with written discourse, and memory and delivery were relegated to oral rhetoric. What once had been a whole theoretical body of rhetoric for some two thousand years was now dissected, with invention, arrangement, and style kept for the composition classroom, while the orphaned memory and delivery were now housed in courses of speech and theater.

The loss of delivery from the writing class also heralded other changes in the academy. By the beginning of the twentieth century, what had been departments of rhetoric increasingly became departments of English literature and rhetoric, or simply English departments. Literature more and more dominated these departments and, eventually, the institutionalization of the two-tier literature and composition system came into vogue. During this time, professors of speech and rhetoric were increasingly ignored by literary scholars and department administrators while reading and writing became the standard of English. More and more academics came to believe that reading and, secondarily, composition were the most important subjects for a liberal education. They jockeyed for more position and power in their departments, edging out those professionals in speech and rhetoric. Therefore, tired of being shunned as the stepchildren of the department, scholars of oral rhetoric seceded from the English union and formed their own separate departments of rhetoric and public speaking (Connors, Ede, Lunsford 5–6), taking with them delivery and memory. Thus, the split of Cicero's five canons was permanent, separated by the political dividing lines of academic departments. Delivery's exile from the rhetorical canon lasted until more recent times when the "process" mode of writing instruction became more common.

RECENT DEVELOPMENTS IN THE THEORY OF DELIVERY

For much of the twentieth century, composition studies ignored rhetorical theory. However, by the 1960s an interest in neo-Aristotelian ideas led the way to viewing rhetoric as public discourse and mutual inquiry. Thus, textbooks began to slowly bring the rhetorical tradition back to composition (Casaregola and Farrar 738). Even so, it was not until the 1990s that the study of rhetorical delivery made a resurgence. Until now, the discussion of delivery (and memory) by textbooks has been, as John Frederick Reynolds states, abandoned, removed, neglected, ignored, limited, simplified, misrepresented, and misunderstood (*Rhetorical* 3). Today, the re-visioning of delivery has become easier due to the "equivalencies between oral, written, and electronic *pronunciatio* and *actio*, something computer-assisted writing has accomplished for some time now" (4). Two other reasons for the revived interest in delivery are the recently renewed emphasis on whole language education—reading, writing, speaking, and listening (Sabio 2); and the study of what Walter Ong terms *secondary orality* (to be discussed later). Therefore, theorists have begun to pay special attention to the role of delivery in the writing process. Here, I want to briefly mention a few of these studies. (Chapter 2 discusses other current theories.)

In *Physical Eloquence and the Biology of Writing*, Robert Ochsner's approach to delivery is along the more physical path in that he stresses a neurological foundation for writing, that is, the eye, hand, and ear needed for composing. Ochsner divides the classical five parts of a successful speech into two groups: the mental processes of invention, arrangement, and style, and the physical processes of memory and delivery. The most basic change he has made is that the order of the five is reversed: delivery, memory, style, arrangement, and invention. He believes that students typically deliver their ideas straight from their brain to the paper. Thus, "delivery changes from the actual presentation of a speech to become the study of hand, eye, and ear" (3–4). Ochsner's theories on the physiology of producing a text, or "delivery," incorporate prewriting and collaborative writing at the beginning stages of a student's composition as rhetorical delivery instead of the traditional presentation of the product at the end of the process.

Likewise, delivery is viewed by Robert Connors, Sam Dragga, and Sheri Helsley as the presentation of the final product, a more physical form of delivery. Connors believes delivery has always existed in the written form as the end product, but currently, writers need no longer conform to the "series of terse, mechanical commandments" that insisted on one-size white bond paper, double-spaced, stapled, and so on. Computers and word processors have opened delivery to different fonts, sizes, and electronic presentations, all of which can essentially affect the readers' disposition toward the writer and message ("*Actio*" 66). Dragga, too, defines delivery as the typographic and illustrative characteristics on a page or screen and believes that advertisers must consider ethical standards when delivering their messages (Dragga 79). Likewise, Helsley states that classical rhetoric prompts us to address the use of electronic technology as delivery in presentation: "We expose our students to the power of presentation in both encoding and decoding—an issue that has largely been ignored in contemporary education" (Helsley 158).

Reynolds also believes that current rhetorical theory recognizes the equivalence of delivery in written and electronic forms—"analogies between voice/gesture and layout/typography." Theories on technical and computer-assisted composition encourage reconsideration of delivery, according to Reynolds ("Delivery" 173).

Similarly, Stephen Bernhardt views delivery as "visual rhetoric….the study of the design of the text on pages…" (746). In this way, the reader or viewer may find the text forbidding or inviting, depending on the way in which it is delivered on the page. Readers must examine the text for visual cues to its meaning: organization, emphasis, beginnings, and endings. "In contrast to the flow of speech, the graphic quality of writing heightens boundaries and discontinuities" (746). Like the aforementioned rhetoricians, Bernhardt states that delivery has been greatly influenced by desktop publishing. Computers, printers, and software give writers full control of the text's appearance, making the text into manipulable objects, movable pieces of language (747).

Even though these theorists—Ochsner, Connors, Dragga, Helsley, Reynolds, and Bernhardt—incorporate some components of the noetic stance, I see their ideas as having more of the physical qualities of delivery. Of course, this is not the traditional physicality of gestures but a contemporary system of what the end product will look like to the reader.

On the other hand, although Kathleen Welch often concentrates on the final physical product, she states that delivery is weakened by many theorists when it is defined only as gestures or, by extension, only as print. Instead, she wants delivery to be given the status of a "medium" because it has been reconstructed through electronic forms of discourse ("Reconfiguring" 21). She believes that "delivery is a site for excavating how forms of discourse have changed the ways rhetoric operates now" ("Reconfiguring" 22). In fact, in her definition of what delivery has meant through rhetorical history, she has included all media:

> In ancient times this canon [delivery] indicated gesture, movement, and other physical issues in oral presentations. With the burgeoning power of literacy and later of secondary orality, it came to signify medium, or symbol system. The ability to perform in any medium. (*Contemporary* 168)

Citing Ong's theories of secondary orality (see chapter 2 for more discussion), Welch claims that "delivery is secondary orality" and textbooks should treat electronic forms of discourse as issues that affect consciousness ("Reconfiguring" 22, 26). The way in which the message is delivered can have a great impact on the receiver of the message. Delivery as secondary orality "…depicts a stage of consciousness rather than the mere use of tools with various skills. . ." ("Reconfiguring" 22). Welch claims that by using delivery as secondary orality, we can empower students through writing by making them and their teachers more conscious of the technology that determines the result of their interpretation of the meaning, and by understanding where media comes from and what it consists of, which shows the students more possibilities of each medium and develops student relationships with the media (Contemporary 156). Given that Welch strongly underlines the consciousness portion of delivery, I have placed her theories on the noetic end of the delivery continuum.

WOMEN'S CHALLENGE TO DELIVERY IN THE RHETORICAL TRADITION

Traditionally, theory about delivery has presumed it to be delivery by a male body. Women, in general, had been barred from public speaking, a condition that has led to difficulty for contemporary researchers. Hence, missing from my preceding discussion of the rhetorical history of delivery are many marginalized voices, those of women (aside from the Delsarte system), of people of color, of non-Western European people. I have scoured what texts I could find for any allusion to a theory of delivery, but have come up empty handed. Women rhetoricians (those whose texts we can find) before the Delsarte era made no direct mention of delivery. This lack of women's theory on delivery could be attributed to their proscription from public speaking. As Mary Astell wrote in 1697, "Women have no business with the Pulpit, the Bar or St. Stephens Chapel: And Nature does for the most part furnish 'em with such a Musical Tone, Perswasive [sic] air and Winning Address as renders their Discourse sufficiently agreeable in Private Conversation" (123). Therefore, women may not have concerned themselves with developing *pronunciatio* skills because they had few, if any, social situations in which such skills were needed. Learned women, then, may also have felt no need to conceptualize a theory of public delivery, or to theorize on how delivery was affected if the speaker was a woman.

To circumvent this roadblock in my research, I have re-visioned delivery so as to include women in this historical survey of delivery in rhetorical theory. My re-visioning takes two forms: first, I have redefined a woman's "public" to include social settings in which women were allowed to speak, for example, the behind-the-scenes maneuvering that would have taken place at palaces and in aristocratic circles during the Renaissance period; second, for later periods, working from spectators' descriptions of women delivering speeches (particularly during the suffragist and civil rights movements), I have extrapolated a theory of delivery from the descriptions. That is, the woman's own delivery style indicated her concept of delivery, if she were to formulate one.

However, in using these two re-visionings, I must sacrifice the basic framework I have used thus far. I am hard pressed to indicate where on the continuum the women's delivery theories fit best because I cannot discern from mere description whether a woman believes delivery is a purely physical act or if delivery is influenced more by noetic processes. I can only describe what is available and how I might interpret those texts.

The first woman I could find who described how a woman should act behind the scenes was Pan Chao, a first century CE Chinese scholar. The only woman to occupy the post of historian to the Imperial Court of China, Pan Chao assumed the duties of instructor to the young empress and her ladies-in-waiting. She wrote narrative poetry, memorials to the throne, and numerous other texts, many of which have been lost to time (xi). In about 106 CE, Pan Chao wrote "Lessons for Women," subtitled "Instructions in Seven Chapters for a Woman's Ordinary Way of Life in the First Century A.D." This treatise on the education of women outlines in detail how women are to conduct themselves throughout their lives.

Her style of writing is very self-effacing and humble, a style that reflects what she propounds for women. Despite the fact that all women should be educated, just as men, Pan Chao stated that a woman's primary duty is to "humble herself before others....Let her bear disgrace; let her even endure when others speak or do evil to her. Always let her seem to tremble and to fear" (83). When a woman speaks, she is "to choose her words with care; to avoid vulgar language; to speak at appropriate times" (86). She went on to list the appropriate times, such as to one's husband, father, mother, or trusted advisor, but never in public. If this is the case, I assume that had Pan Chao written a treatise on delivery, she would state that women were to speak at the appropriate times (which in most cases would be in private to her husband) and with the appropriate, demure physical movements and gestures of a humble wife. At the same time, because she was so sensitive to the context in which a woman should speak, I believe Pan Chao would also be reluctant to use any set of rigid rules to govern delivery. Instead, the context would signal the delivery.

Another of the earliest women to talk about behind-the-scenes maneuvering is Christine de Pizan. Her father was court astrologer and encouraged de Pizan's education while in Paris, in spite of her mother's opposition. When de Pizan was widowed at 25 years of age, she turned to writing in order to support her three small children. In *A Medieval Woman's Mirror of Honor: The Treasury of the City of Ladies* (1405), she outlined the politically effective uses of oral language for a female ruler, recommending she use speech primarily in private, not public, settings. In fact, all public actions should be performed for a female ruler by surrogates, male advisors who speak for her, although de Pizan believed the best alternative is a husband who can speak for the princess (90–94, 168–170). I assume that she equated speaking in public as intimately connected to a loss of chastity and other womanly "virtues."

She also particularly recommended a pacifist role for the female ruler, encouraging her to be the peacemaker between her husband and any warring barons: "Gentleness and humility assuage the prince. The gentle tongue (which means the soft word) bends and breaks harshness. So water extinguishes fire's heat by its moisture and chill" (86). Thus, if a princess is to make peace with a gentle tongue, presumably her words would be delivered in the same manner.

At all times, de Pizan repeated that a woman's speech must be yet another inducement for people to like her. This was her advice for all classes of women: ruling, merchant, artisan, and servants. She seemed to insist that the only way a woman can make gains in her life is to be kind, giving, and peaceful. Even in times of aggression from neighboring barons, the princess is to speak to her men-at-arms in a way to promote loyalty and their best efforts (170).

Thus, if de Pizan formulated a concept of delivery for women, I conclude that she would state that no matter who the audience is, a princess should ever be mindful of remaining a "Lady," not only as the title but in every sense of the word. She must be demure and gentle in words and in bearing, not making any undue gestures or movements unsuitable to her title.

As I mentioned earlier, Mary Astell was not in favor of women speaking in public, but she argued that education is the natural right of all thinking people. She was educated by her clergyman uncle, Ralph Astell, and campaigned throughout her life in defense of female education and the necessity to resist tyranny, especially in marriage. Education without public speaking seems to be antithetical. Even so, like her two predecessors de Pizan and Pan Chao, Astell was raised with the premise that women were not public creatures. Instead, their domain was the home. Any public business was handled strictly by men—husbands, fathers, brothers, uncles, or guardians. Thus, being bred with such a social restriction, Astell most likely saw no place for women in public.

On the other hand, despite her admonitions against women public speakers, she did allude to delivery in one short note in her *A Serious Proposal to the Ladies* (1694). When commenting on the distinction between speaking and writing, Astell stated, "they Talk best who mingle Solidity of Thought with th' agreeableness of a ready Wit.... [I]t takes more with some

Auditors many times than Good Sense" (123). In other words, good sense alone is not always enough to persuade an audience. Instead, an effective speaker also has to use wit, for instance, delivery, to read an audience, to get their attention, to stir up their emotions. Unfortunately, given the brevity of this statement, it is difficult to extrapolate any particular theory of delivery.

At this point, one issue should be addressed: de Pizan and Astell were White women, and this tradition of publicly silenced, educated women may have been strictly a White woman's tradition. Though we have no way of knowing, or at least very little evidence as to whether women of color spoke out publicly before the 1800s, we do know that African-American women blazed the trail for other women in the public forum. This led the way, in the mid1800s, to White women coming out from those behind-the-scenes contexts and beginning to make themselves heard publicly.

Probably the first woman to speak publicly to men and women, Maria W. Miller Stewart was one of America's first African-American woman political writers. According to Marilyn Richardson, Stewart, during her three-year tenure of speaking in Boston (1831–33), was a bold and militant orator in defense of women's rights (xiii). Stewart's voice was "full of assurance, spirit, energy, creative imagination and fervor" and much of her technique was taken from religious orators of the time (14, 15). Therefore, Stewart's idea of delivery would most likely incorporate a call-and-response cadence of African-American preachers.

Following in Stewart's footsteps, Sojourner Truth began her public-speaking career in 1843. She was a former slave, with no formal education, but according to descriptions of her speeches, she had a great rhetorical ability to stir up emotions in an audience (Campbell, vol. I 33). From the texts of her speeches, we can see that she, too, employed a call-and-response technique similar to that of Stewart. For instance, in her "Ain't I a Woman?" speech in Akron, Ohio (1851), her text reflects the influence of call-and-response:

> Then they talk about this thing in the head; what this they call it? [Intellect, someone whispers.] That's it, honey. What that got to do with women's rights or negro's rights? If my cup won't hold but a pint, and your holds a quart, wouldn't you be mean not to let me have my little half-measure full? (cited in Schneir 95)

With the cadence of her speeches, the delivery style that Truth employed may be called indicative of her cultural background, as with Stewart.

A key organizer for East Coast labor strikes, Elizabeth Gurley Flynn also spent her life as a leader of free-speech battles. Her speaking career began in 1905 when she won an award in her grammar school debating society for urging that women be given the vote. Even then, Flynn's oratorical style was being touted by the press:

> Elizabeth Gurley Flynn hypnotized the crowd before she had got far in her discourse. She has an odd manner of making what might be called short hand gestures, pot hooks, curves, dots and dashes written in the air. Soon they [audience] were frowning when she frowned, laughing when she laughed, growing terribly earnest when she grew moderately so. (cited in Braxandall 75)

According to descriptions, Flynn gave fiery orations of tremendous energy: "I know how to get the power out of my diaphragm instead of my vocal chords" (cited in Braxandall 10), and her niece described her speaking voice as "downright scary—rich, full, and magnificent" (cited in Braxandall 70). Flynn also made great use of hand gestures: "Eight fingers for an eight hour day, a fist for unity, a few fingers for the offerings of management, many for the wages demanded by strikers" (cited in Braxandall 10). If I were to speculate on a theory of delivery for Flynn, it would have to include many hand gestures and vocal control in order to sway an audience.

In contrast, Margaret Fuller believed in the conversational delivery of speech. Fuller, an advocate for women's rights, particularly for birth control, was also a teacher in the late 1830s at an all-girls school. Whereas the boys were trained in both rhetoric and elocution and twice monthly declaimed before the entire school, Fuller trained her girls not for public declamation, but to provide them with practical tools though which to communicate clearly (Kolodny 144). She intended the exchanges to be "social and pleasant" (cited in H. Johnson 135). Employing the conversational method, Fuller generated calls for accuracy and definition in the group's shared pursuit for meaning through words (Kolodny 145).

Thus, if Fuller had determined a theory of delivery, certainly it would have been the opposite of the flamboyant Flynn. Fuller incorporated a conversational tone, with few gestures, in an attempt to engage her audience in a mutual exchange of ideas.

Despite restrictions from public speaking, many women at this time formulated a type of "feminine style" in their orations. Karlyn Kohrs Campbell describes such a style in her two-volume rhetorical study of public speeches and writings by White and African-American women in the nineteenth century:

On the one hand, a woman had to meet all the usual requirements of speakers, demonstrating expertise, authority, and rationality in order to show her competence and make herself credible to audiences. However, if that was all she did, she was likely to be judged masculine, unwomanly, aggressive and cold. As a result, women speakers sometimes searched for ways to legitimate such "unwomanly" behavior and for ways to incorporate evidence of femininity into ordinary rhetorical action. (vol. I 12)

Women needed to overcome the fact that they were seen as unfeminine because they spoke in public. Thus, as Campbell states, they tried to find ways in which to emphasize, while speaking, what society believed to be "feminine" qualities. Therefore, I suggest that the delivery of a feminine-style speech was in a self-effacing, demur physical manner, similar to the one that de Pizan recommends for behind the scenes. These qualities were seen by the public (largely men) as reflecting "true womanhood."

Even rhetoric and composition textbooks written by women at the turn of the century did not mention any theories of delivery. Women rhetoricians such as Gertrude Buck and Sara Lockwood in their textbooks gave detailed outlines of how to write a persuasive speech or engage in a heated debate. Yet, these women did not touch on any theory of how to use either the voice or the gestures needed to perform such a task. Again, I must surmise that because women had been proscribed from public speaking, even women teachers and writers did not know how to go about doing so. Having had no training in delivery, these professional women did not know how to formulate such a theory (or did not dare to go against society's rule to do so).

CONCLUSION

Rhetorical history at times gives us quite different views of delivery, some from theory and others from mere observation of how rhetoricians spoke. Delivery has meant only physical movement, a hand gesture, a look, a tilt of the head, or print on a page, and delivery has also meant the noetic processes that influenced that gesture, look, head tilt, or how those pages were filled. More important, despite the tension between the physical and noetic theories, delivery has survived over the centuries, even after some theorists tried to cut it entirely from every rhetorical canon. My contention is that delivery should continue to survive and flourish in the writing classroom alongside invention, arrangement, style, and memory. Therefore, in the next chapter, I bring to light facets of delivery that exist in today's writing theories and polish those facets, giving writing a new theory of delivery.

2

Defining and Redefining Delivery

As described in the previous chapter, the centuries-old tension between the noetic and physical theories of delivery caused a rift in the rhetorical canon. Delivery was banished to places beyond the English classroom, that is, to speech and theater departments, and stayed in exile until the contemporary writing process evolved. Theorists claimed that after centuries of dispute, delivery was not relevant to writing classes; therefore, only the application of invention, arrangement, and style was left for struggling students, leaving a hole that I believe has constricted writing theory.

Nonetheless, aspects of delivery can be seen in a variety of practices currently used in writing classes: debates, role-playing, town meetings, and simply reading aloud to peers, teachers, or both. These practices have rarely been discussed from the perspective of delivery and the classical rhetorical canon. Some bodies of theory, though, do exist in related areas, specifically oral versus written discourse, collaboration, audience awareness, performance, and the feminist practice of "writing the body." Not only do these areas refer to the noetic aspects of delivery but also to its physical attributes as described in chapter 1. Accordingly, for the remainder of this chapter, I plan to discuss these areas of current writing theory and practices, along with some new approaches to theory that have not yet been applied to the writing classroom. Then, I want to synthesize these recent theories in order to move toward a re-visioned theory of delivery.

SPEAKING AND WRITING

According to feminist Gabriel Josipovici, writing and speaking are at the crossroads of the mental and the physical, the orders of culture and of nature

(1). In the previous chapter, I developed a continuum on which delivery moved from a purely physical aspect (Cicero) to a more noetic aspect (Bacon). Using Josipovici's statement, we can place writing and speaking on that continuum of delivery: writing has most often been identified as a purely noetic process, whereas speaking is associated more with the physical. With this in mind, it is easy to see which aspects of delivery are associated with writing (noetic) and speaking (physical), but both writing and speaking must involve overlapping noetic and physical processes. If we attempt to divorce one from the other, the noetic from the physical, we have neither, or at best, we have a static choreographed set of motions, such as Austin's elocution rules. Once again, we are left without a complete theory of delivery for the writing classroom. Hence, in order to reinstate delivery in the classroom, speaking must also be reintegrated with writing, the physical with the noetic, in teaching strategies. Therefore, contemporary theories on oral versus written discourse are an integral part of a re-visioned theory of delivery.[1]

For centuries, there has been an argument over which is primary, speech or writing. John Schafer states that Greeks dating from the third century BCE claimed that written language was supreme, and to no surprise, their system of phonetics was letter-based. On the other side of the issue is Ferdinand de Saussure, who argued that speech had the main role and that writing is only a way of recording language by means of visible marks. Both these views were challenged by J. Vachek, who argued that neither writing nor speaking is primary; they are functionally complementary systems. In some situations, writing serves a society's communication needs best; in other situations, speech does (Schafer 3). Even earlier, at the turn of this century, Fred Newton Scott and Joseph Villiers Denney challenged contemporary rhetoric by saying that spoken and written discourse should be

---

[1]An aside to the discussion of speaking and writing is Walter Ong's theory of primary and secondary orality. Primary orality is the pristine orality untouched by writing or print in areas sheltered from the full impact of literacy. Secondary orality is induced by radio and television, which are totally dependent on writing and print for their existence. As examples of such cultures, Ong points to our own urban areas. The distinctively oral culture of African-American urban ghettos and some isolated rural areas are basically primary oral cultures in many ways, though more or less modified by contact with secondary orality today. On the other hand, generally, the orality of nonghetto urban populations and of suburbia, White and Black, is basically secondary orality (132–33). Because of these two types of orality, we must make students aware of what oral speech is and what writing is by contrast. Delivery here could play an even larger role because students from oral cultural backgrounds would be more adept at delivering their ideas orally rather than in a written form. As Glenda E. Gill states, "The written word, for many, is the language of an unknown tongue" (225). Thus, beyond the skills-building need to rejoin speaking and writing, a teacher must be able to reinforce both written and oral delivery in the classroom in order to not shut out part of the population. (For more discussion of delivery and secondary orality, see Kathleen Welch's *The Contemporary Reception of Classical Rhetoric: Appropriations of Ancient Discourse* and "Reconfiguring Writing and Delivery in Secondary Orality.")

reunited. They believed that spoken discourse is valuable training for the writer because it involves addressing an actual audience, requiring students to shape their messages for a particular group of individuals. Speech requires that the orator consider others, their uniqueness and variety, in the communication act. This, in turn, they stated, improves writing, teaching students to respond to their audience not as a set of abstract faculties, as with classical rhetoric, but as whole human beings (Berlin, *Writing Instruction* 82). Thus, both the noetic and the physical aspects of delivery are called on when combining speech and writing.

As proof of this speaking and writing connection, we can turn to Janet Emig, who also acknowledges the need to rejoin oral and written discourse. She quotes a study by Anthony Tovatt that focused on process writing as opposed to product. The study proceeded from the premise that "we write with our ears" and that if students can hear what they are writing, and if they can deliver their work to themselves as an audience, they can transmute satisfactory patterns of written discourse. In this study, students not only saw, but also heard, what was being delivered onto the paper through teacher modeling or through audio-active headsets. Tovatt's findings revealed that in the first year, students showed general superiority over conventional approaches to increasing student writing abilities (cited in Emig 20). For this case, writing with their ears and hearing what was being done through oral delivery resulted in better writing. Although this is only one case of research, it does uphold the need for teachers to reintegrate speaking with writing.

Likewise, John Schafer advocates a rejoining of oral to written discourse, particularly because developmental writers have mastered the complex grammar of speech dialogue (27) but are uncomfortable with writing. As in a conversation, they know how to produce a text in cooperation with a partner through noetic and physical delivery. However, they cannot initiate the text, prolong it, and bring it to a close unassisted by another person because there is no delivery to an audience and, thus, no feedback. The difficulty comes because conversational dialogues are different from essay dialogues. When simply conversing with someone, especially with a friend, the speaker does not need to be explicit because the individuals share a great deal of knowledge. Hints and code words suffice in getting the message across. However, the type of dialogue needed for a text is, as Schafer puts it, more like a talk-show host with a guest; the purpose is to produce a text that a third party (the television audience) will find understandable and interesting (27). Practice in sharing written texts orally with students can alleviate part of this problem. Students hear the written texts spoken and internalize the skills needed for their own writing, thus rejoining speaking and writing.

Similarly, Dorothy Augustine and W. Ross Winterowd consider the hypothetical responses projected by a writer as a correlate to conversational cues (silent and spoken) that speakers constantly receive from listeners during delivery. As they state, speakers know whether to continue speaking, stop to explain something, back up, or skip ahead because of listeners' verbal and nonverbal signals. The signals can be blunt—a listener interrupts—or subtle—a listener's dilated pupils as silent affirmation of what is being said. In other words, the listener is delivering cues to the speaker who is delivering the words. In the writer–reader relationship, there is no such transaction, and this may be the most fundamental reason for the writer to invent an audience, to project hypothetical responses that indicate the audience's response to the writing (128). Yet, less-skilled students have a difficult time inventing a silent audience. They need those verbal and nonverbal cues of a live audience. Therefore, through combining speaking with writing, teachers provide a real audience for students. Conversations in classrooms between peers are full of requests for clarification and elaboration, thus helping the writer to physically see and hear an audience. The dialogic relationship between speech and writing characterizes writing groups because the participants combine the two, a speaker delivering and an audience responding.

In the same manner, James L. Collins states that in spoken dialogue, meaning is the creation of more than one person; as speaker and listener roles shift, participants may alternately contribute to the construction of meaning (198). Hence, meaning is established through cooperation and collaboration, a back-and-forth delivery. Along with sharing the construction of meaning, the conversants also share features of the linguistic environment that supports and contributes to meaning: gestures, facial expressions, pitch, intonation, and contexts of situation and culture. On the other hand, in writing, these shared features of meaning diminish or disappear entirely. Writing is produced by one person alone and, if the audience is not intimately known, there are no shared referential contexts. As a result, writing must represent meaning more fully than does speaking. All that is meaningful in conversation, including nonverbally shared dialogue, must be adequately stated when writing. Collins summarizes, "Speaking and writing, in short, represent meaning in different ways" (198–99). Yet, speaking and writing cannot function separately. Student writers must first learn what is needed in spoken dialogue before they are able to recreate conversation on paper.

Unfortunately, weak writers produce essays as if readers will cooperate and collaborate to produce meaning, as do participants in spoken conversations. For conversants, the assumption that language is supplemented by unspoken contexts that support and complete the structuring of meaning works well. They know it works in conversation, but without considering the fact that the delivery of the content to the audience has changed drastically in the leap from oral to written discourse, developmental writers assume it will work in their essays. As Collins says, "What is elaborated meaning in speaking becomes abbreviated meaning in writing, meaning that points toward, but does not explicitly represent, contextual referents" (199). Consequently, weak writers merely deliver their ideas onto the paper without contexts, without anticipating an audience's questions and situations. Therefore, the construction of meaning through a combination of speaking and writing, the physical and the noetic, should be placed as primary in the writing classroom.

Although many contemporary theorists advocate oral discourse in a writing class, Robert Ochsner points out the dangers of this practice. He believes that speech and prose differ in their production and delivery and admonishes that it is important for students to understand (at least intuitively) the problem of using a speech-based rhythm for generating writing. Yet, the same rhythm enhances readability because it establishes a relatively quick, familiar, and predictable pace for interpretation. Thus, contrastively, writing and speaking define one rhythm and potentially share the other (98–99). Ochsner claims that it is a social amenity to guide the reader by signaling a consistent and appropriate rhythm for interpretation. This rhythm guides the audience, as would physical cueing in a conversation. Thus, students can acquire this skill by practicing the conversational rhythms used for speech, something that is relatively easy to develop through the practice of reading aloud. "In other words, students can learn to read aloud with emphasis, attentive to the pauses that different authors require, and ultimately to the interpretive rhythm of their own prose" (101). That is, delivering prose aloud to an audience is good practice for the delivering of written prose onto paper.

Unfortunately, Ochsner continues, by adopting a speech production pace, developmental writers often generate speech-like vocabulary. Their discourse focuses on the "I" point of view and other characteristics of writer-based prose. These features of speech become serious problems for developmental writers who depend too much on spoken language to express their ideas. Their dependence is signaled by inappropriate speech-to-prose transfers, often too informal for academic writing (89). Ochsner's solution to this problem is a style called "spoken prose." Prose that reads well, in spoken-prose style, aligns a text with speech for ease of interpretation, for the quicker, more speech-like timing of language processing (88). He claims that in terms of production speed, speaking and thinking are closely matched processes, bringing together both the noetic and the physical aspects of delivery through a linking of oral and written discourse.

Walter Ong also points to the differences between writing and speaking and our need to combine them for teaching strategies. He states, "Writing is completely and irremediably artificial and that what you find in the dictionary are not real words but coded marks for voicing real words, exteriorly or in imagination.... Speech is structured through the entire fabric of the human person. Writing depends on consciously contrived rules" (129). Thus, moving from this natural oral world into an artificial world of writing is frightening, especially to beginners, and teachers in traditional classrooms are no help. The silence, broken only by pens scratching or keys typing, only reinforces the fear of putting words on paper. If students could first deliver their ideas to an audience, using noetic and physical delivery, they could receive reactions and encouragement, lessening their fear. As it stands, too often students are left to their own devices. When this occurs, as Thomas Farrell says, students encounter two basic problems when attempting to move from orality to writing: developmental writers make assertions that are totally unsupported by reasons, and they make a series of statements that want connections (Ong 131). Because students lack an audience for their delivery, they receive no feedback by which to judge their work and are, therefore, prone to such problems as faulty logic and missed connections. In order to alleviate such problems, teachers need to combine speaking with writing, providing the students with an audience for feedback.

With such practice, Barry Kroll maintains, the students' writing and speaking abilities mature, becoming more extensive, or overlapping, in their potential uses. For mature communicators, speaking and writing have parallel purposes. For instance, they can talk "writing" (create a relatively autonomous and explicit oral text to be physically delivered through speech) and write "talking" (create a written utterance that is heavily dependent on shared knowledge not explicitly represented in the written product). Kroll believes that when oral and written resources are systematically integrated, not simply consolidated, an individual can make choices within a flexible, organized system of voices, registers, and styles most appropriate for the purpose, audience, and context of communication (53). This also includes a choice of delivery style—whether it be written (delivered onto paper or computer screen) or spoken (formally or casually). With Kroll's theory, students eventually combine the noetic and the physical as a matter of habit, internalizing a complete practice of delivery.

Some theorists have praised the value of speaking in a writing class, and many contemporary classrooms make use of speaking as an invention tool. In fact, we can see traces of traditional delivery in some contemporary theories, such as those of Ochsner, Emig, and Ong, but overall, the writing class remains silent. Written language descends from an oral tradition that incorporated physical and noetic delivery, and like them, writing and speaking complement each other. As the survey on speaking and writing theory has shown, oral and written compositions are both important halves of delivery. They are at the crossroads of the mental and physical, as Josipovici states, but they cannot be separated without damage to one of them. From the beginning of language, without speaking, there would have been no writing. In other words, speaking must be an integral part of the entire writing process. We can accomplish this through a re-visioned theory of delivery.

DIALOGUE

The word *dialogue* has been used metaphorically by composition theorists to indicate how teaching writing is about helping prepare students to "converse" in their later lives, in other disciplines, at work, and so on. However, I would like to draw attention back to the literal meaning of that metaphor, dialogue: a talking together aloud, an interchange of ideas, especially when seeking mutual understanding or harmony. We may see that the modern classroom is more active than the traditional one, but basically, students still create their essays in silence, on their own, using merely their brains and hands. Instead, I believe, like Kenneth Bruffee's "Collaboration and 'The *Conversation* of Mankind'" (emphasis added), that a writing classroom should be one in which there is conversation, a delivery of dialogue in an effort to reunite the physical body and the intellect. With this intent in mind, I want to discuss current theories of collaboration and audience.

Theories underlying the collaborative movement in education contend that because knowledge is socially constructed or generated, collaborative interactions in class can lead to new knowledge or learning. This view is opposed to the hierarchical theory that knowledge must be imparted by a designated "knower" to those less informed.

One of the leading proponents of social constructionism is Bruffee, who describes collaborative learning as providing a "community in which normal discourse occurs…a context in which students can practice and master the normal discourse exercised in established knowledge communities in the academic world and in business, government, and the professions" (642). He states that students who are without membership in certain discourse communities they wish to enter can help one another because no student is "wholly ignorant and inexperienced" (644). Education for Bruffee is a process of learning to take part in the conversation of humanity, and "collaborative learning is an arena in which students can negotiate their way into that conversation" (647). Teachers can enable this movement into the conversation by utilizing collaborative groups in class. Peer voices that students hear delivering conversation in their collaborative groups contribute to what the students internalize and later use in writing.

Taken one step further, the conversation from such small groups can be molded into written discourse. As Bruffee states, "writing is at once two steps away from conversation and a return to conversation. We converse; we internalize conversation as thought; and then by writing, we re-immerse conversation in its external, social medium" (641). Therefore, to Bruffee, whether students are writing separately or in groups on one project, the writing remains a collaboration, a social act similar to that of delivering a speech to an audience.

Anne Ruggles Gere supports Bruffee's theories by borrowing from Lev Vygotsky and Mikhail Bakhtin. She states that if we accept language as a social construction and the "sense" of words emerges from their surrounding context, then dialogue becomes more than preliminary to writing: "it is essential to the whole activity: essential because the language writers use depends upon their social participation, and peer response provides a specialized society for writers" (88). In collaboration groups, the writers do more than offer one another helpful advice; they exchange meanings. Thus, Gere states that the dialogue of peer groups gives life to Bakhtin's claim that "words are always half of someone else's by putting writers in a context where they create language as part of their dialogue with others" (88). Thus, the act of delivery becomes a two-way exchange, with the orator or writer giving one side of the text from his or her noetic abilities through physical action and the audience responding through the dialogue.

Similarly, Karen Burke LeFevre writes that rhetorical invention/creation "is better understood as a social act which an individual who is at the same time a social being interacts in a distinctive way with society and culture to create something" (1). This rhetorical act of invention/creation, whether written or spoken, has two parts: the commencement of the creative act and the reception or execution of it (or the delivery thereof). Thus, as LeFevre states, the writer or speaker requires the presence of the "other." Possibly, this other may be the rhetor herself, another side of her internalized self conceived from social experience, or it may be an actual audience of others. It may be a collaborator who has helped with the creation or a reader whose participation in the text completes the enterprise (38). In any instance, the delivery is not complete unless there is the presence of the other.

However, Richard Johannesen believes that for dialogue there must be face-to-face oral communication: "Dialogue is unlikely to occur in writing or in mass media situations" (381–382). This is in opposition to LeFevre's stance that a writer may be in dialogue with an inner self that has been socialized through experience. Like other composition theorists, Johannesen defines communication as dialogue rather than as monologue. He believes that in dialogue, the essential movement is "turning toward, outgoing to, and reaching for the other. And a basic element in dialogue is 'seeing the other' or 'experiencing the other side'" (375). Yet, whether to have that face-to-face situation or to gain experience to form that inner socialized self, writers must have an audience. The audience may be the writer herself, or it may be a million people who read a daily newspaper, or the thirty people of a class, or the three people in a collaborative group. To be completed, the delivery must be to the other.

At the same time, the individuals that make up that audience are diverse; they hold difference values and opinions. As Richard Young, Alton Becker, and Kenneth Pike state, though, human differences are the raw material of writing: "They are our reason for wishing to communicate. Through communication we create community.... To do so, we must overcome the barriers to communication that are, paradoxically, the motive for communication" (30). Therefore, the writer must build bridges across those differences. Before doing so, the writer must understand what she and the audience have in common, what features they share in order to communicate. According to Young, Becker, and Pike, when the writer knows the audience well (a relative, a friend, a business associate), then she can deliver her message easily; they speak the same language. On the other hand, when the audience is less known to the writer, difficulties can occur because the writer must anticipate the audience's responses before delivering her ideas. If the writer fails to anticipate them correctly, then she may fail to communicate (178). Here is where the teacher can help the student writer through peer groups. The physically present audience can give immediate reaction to the student writer, indicating whether she has communicated the message. Granted, these are all students, most likely not professionals. Nonetheless, they can role-play other audiences and, eventually, the student writer will internalize these different social groups and be able to progress from addressing the small, known audience (like herself) to addressing a distant, unknown, and different audience.

Likewise, Moffett agrees that an immediate audience is imperative to the writing process. He claims that learning to use language "requires the particular feedback of human response, because it is to other people that we direct speech. The fact that one writes by oneself does not at all diminish the need for response, since one writes for others" (*Universe*, 191). However, he also firmly believes that the teacher is the wrong audience. He has found that peers are a natural audience; students write much better when they do so for their peers. Teachers are usually seen as the authority, the wielder of grades, a role that distorts the writer–audience relationship. Consequently, the student may misuse the comments given by a teacher in ways that severely limit learning to write. That is, the writer may try to write "what the teacher wants" or even what she doesn't want, or a student may shrug off a teacher's comments as English instructors being too nitpicky. If peers misread the intent—the message—then she must accommodate that reaction. Moffett claims this may not be universally true, and students may act in similarly irrelevant ways toward peers. However, in general, peers are a more effective audience. If the teacher shifts authority to the peer group (which is where it lies anyway), taking an indirect role, then her feedback carries a greater weight (194). Another advantage of peer audiences is that by habitually responding and coaching each other, students get more insights into their own writing. Thus, the role of the teacher, Moffett claims, is to teach the students to teach each other (196). Through a back-and-forth delivery of ideas in peer groups, students can be the ideal audience/teachers for the speaker/writer.

Similarly, George Yoos concludes that the ideal audience generates questions, setting up a framework of queries and possible interpretations that force writers to explain their aims and the meaning of what they say. "The audience role looks at what promotes the interest and attention of the reader" (247). Writers need to anticipate and eliminate ambiguities that may interfere with audience comprehension. To perform such a feat, writers must be able to conjure up the ideal critical audience to whom to deliver their text. However, students often have no idea of how to accomplish this magic. Therefore, having an audience physically present to either listen to or read their writings is good practice for forming that internalized audience. The physically present, critical audience will point out possible misconstructions, misreadings, misinterpretations, or misunderstandings that less-experienced student writers may miss.

So, to help students overcome their lack of experience in reaching audiences, they need practice with physically present audiences. Eventually, writers learn to think in the manner of their readers, understanding the reasons behind audience demands. As Peter Smagorinsky states, students who learn to assume the role of their audience gain benefits in understanding constraints and adjusting their writings accordingly. Likewise, students who respond to other student writings provide much more objective comments to guide revision (35). In addition, peer groups as audiences can guide writers through all the steps of text production, from the noetic to the physical processes of delivering the text.

Gere confirms that another benefit of collaboration is that the conversation within writing groups blurs the distinction between writer and audience. "Writing group participants become both writer and audience, incorporating the 'otherness' of the audience into their own writing. In the process, both writers and audience become members of the same language community" (84). This in itself solves many of the overarching problems for student writers (or writers, in general): lack of audience awareness. Here, again, delivery is a two-way process: the speaker or writer delivering the text and the audience delivering its response. When a peer states, "I don't understand," a student writer has learned more than any instructor's comment can provide. Responding to the audience's questions and breaking through the alienation can inspire a student to find more effective ways to deliver ideas.

Due to such enlightening theories, collaboration, once thought of as cheating in school, has become a boom to writing classes. When successful, collaboration in small groups enables the students to accept responsibility for their own work, obtain reactions from their peers, and gain experience for life. Unfortunately, the boom of collaboration in the writing classroom has not gone much beyond its use for revisions. In 1980, Richard Gebhardt, noting that most class groups were utilized mainly for responding to previously composed student drafts, called for the widening of collaboration in writing classes. However, in 1988, Margaret Fleming wrote that there is little evidence that such a broadening has taken place. In fact, the very names of "editing groups" and "response groups" suggest collaboration's limited function. She would like to see students collaborate from the very beginning of their writing task through the final product (78). So it is with delivery, a practice that could incorporate dialogue (collaboration and audience) at every step of the writing process.

Through contemporary interactive classrooms, again, we see that some teachers have attempted to combine the noetic (writing) and the physical (speaking) in an effort to reincorporate the concept of delivery with writing theory. By its very definition—a talking aloud—dialogue may be the essence of delivery in writing classrooms. An interactive process for delivery is established through which students learn to know their audience, how to communicate with them, and how to respond when it is their turn to be an audience member.

PERFORMANCE

Theories on aspects of speaking versus writing, on collaboration, and on audience have all informed the most accepted practices in English writing classrooms today. We have seen how facets of classical delivery still haunt these theories, although delivery for the most part has been divorced from these classrooms for a century. As stated before, delivery has most often been associated with speech and theater departments, and it is to these departments that some English instructors have looked for new practices for their writing classrooms. For example, practices such as role-playing and debating are common in writing classes for invention purposes. Still, I believe that theories of performance and drama can be more fully employed in a re-visioned delivery.

Of course, merely by its nature, drama is the essence of physical delivery, actors/performers revealing their texts through motion and, but not necessarily, through sound. Additionally, if the actors are improvising, not using an already developed text, then the noetic processes of delivery are employed even more. Hence, performance offers teachers a strategy to complement the mostly noetic delivery of writing with a more physical delivery.

Besides borrowing the actual practices of the theater, writing theorists have also borrowed terminology, which we have seen previously. Writing instructors speak of roles, performance, and actors when discussing authorship and audiences. It is my contention that much of the metaphorical terms, just as that of dialogue, should be given back their literal meanings and be combined with dramatic theory to enhance delivery in the writing classroom. With all of this in mind, I have devoted the next section of this chapter to current drama theory in combination with theories by writing instructors who advocate "performance" of some kind in their classrooms, thereby rejoining the physical aspects of delivery to the more noetic. Thus, I believe that by borrowing performance theory from theater and speech and utilizing it in the writing classroom, we may be one step closer to reinstating delivery to its rightful place as part of the whole theory of writing.

The most well-known use of the word *dramatism*, when associated with communication, is attributed to Kenneth Burke, whose theories have inspired many studies over the years. In his *Grammar of Motives*, Burke contends that the basic forms of thought are exemplified in the attributing of motives, and he uses five key terms, collectively called dramatism, as generating principles: act, scene, agent, agency, and purpose. *Act* is defined as naming what took place, in thought or deed. *Scene* names the background of the act, the situation in which it occurred. The person or kind of person who performed the act is the *agent*, the means or instruments he or she used is the *agency*, and *purpose* is the reason behind the act. Burke claims that all human actions may be investigated or simplified by this pentad of terms that are understandable at a glance. "They need never to be abandoned, since all statements that assign motives can be shown to arise out of them and to terminate in them" (x). Burke chose the word *dramatism* to define his pentad because being developed from the analysis of drama, it treats language and thought primarily as modes of action (xvi). For his purposes, Burke used the term *dramatism* in a nonphysical sense. His pentad has not been utilized to define a physical action, only an action in a text.

Utilizing Burke's pentad, Joseph Comprone applies dramatism to writing with a step-by-step process. For instance, he claims that prewriting activities would likely concentrate on agent (writer) and scene (experiential context) as they evolved toward purpose in self-expressive or reflexive terms. This text that ideally would come at the close of this early stage of writing would take on the perspective of a writer addressing herself about a defined area of experience, a type of internal monologue. This monologue, overheard by a teacher and peers, would become the basis for a plan or outline that would, in turn, initiate the second stage of composing, writing for readers (337).

Comprone continues his examination to the final stage of the writing process that is of the most interest to this text. He states that at the final stage of composing, writers must come to see writing as an "acting-together." "In partaking together in the act of reading and writing, individuals must share 'sensations, concepts, images, ideas and attitudes'" (340). As Burke believed, writing is a process of sharing. So, Comprone believes that the audience and writer share equally in the process. Therefore, if we were to use acting-together in a more physical sense, students would share their writing through more than just a sheet of paper. With re-visioned delivery, students perform their writing for an audience and a physicality is added to Burke's theory by which students open dialogues at each step of the noetic writing process.

Another theorist who borrows terms from drama is Robert Brooke, who believes likewise that besides separating the mind functions from the body, writing also removes the author from the audience, dividing the real person from the one conveyed in print, and produces a split between the normal self and the one "staged" by the written text. However, this may be to the advantage of the writer who actually has much of the same opportunities as an actor to invent an identity. She can move from one identity to another according to the circumstances of the writing, normally to suit the appropriate audience. Through interplay of audience and self-identity, a writer can adjust language to fit an audience (29). Brooke states that a playful writer takes risks shifting roles until the right one is adopted. He says that, in addition, the playful writer challenges readers to judge the performance by standards that are not strictly functional. "In this respect...she engages the audience in a game of language play that is won or lost by consensus, according to unstated rules of good taste, style, and eloquence" (31). Through delivery combining the physical and the noetic, the writer can actually test that interplay of language to see when or if she can win a consensus and with which words she is most successful.

In addition, Brooke states that perhaps the most important aspect of learning to write may be identifying and understanding what roles a person will take on as a writer. Writing is meaningful for a person when it supports an attempt to be a certain kind of person in the world, for instance, to be a reflective adult, a persuasive contributor in a debate, or a successful professional:

> For students in writing workshops, the opportunity to explore writers' roles is what prompts their learning. When they can escape the notion that writing is only a means for showing a teacher what they have learned...then they can begin to explore how different roles for themselves as writers might enhance other parts of their lives. (10)

Brooke uses the term *identity negotiations* to define the development of the self within a complex arena of competing social forces. His theory suggests that an individual comes to experience herself as one sort of person rather than another largely through involvement in the social situations that surround her (12). These social situations and groups that surround her are many: family, friends, schools, political parties, religious organizations, and so on. There is no such thing as one single unified social context surrounding the self. Instead, each person lives life in overlapping contexts, each of which requires different practices. Similarly, in the writing classroom, certain roles are established for participants and each will respond to those roles by developing particular versions of them (18–19). The traditional role, as in other classrooms, is that of student, with its accompanying appropriate behavior. Therefore, it is the teacher's job to delimit the students' range of roles in the writing classroom.

As Brooke states, learning to write becomes important when it stems from writers' roles that enhance a student's sense of social self. Hence, teachers need to create environments where writers' roles can connect directly to situations students care about. "Our students' ability to write, their motivation to write, and their effectiveness when writing in contexts beyond our classrooms all depend on students developing such writers' roles" (27). As a result of extending writers' roles beyond the narrow classroom, students can begin to use writing as a means of addressing other roles they face (ethnic, gender, class personal, professional, etc.), but they need the opportunity to test such possible roles in the safety of the classroom. Performance of their writing can offer them such a chance. Through the combining of a physical delivery (performance) with a noetic delivery (writing), students can test the roles they may be expected to play in and out of class.

Expanding on the idea of writer and audience roles, George Yoos writes that both the reader/listener and writer/speaker perform in roles defined by four topics, and if one role is generally accentuated in any specific situation, it is clear that accommodation or sensitivity to all roles can provide a highly enriched perspective on writing (Keith 357). The four topics, or levels, that define these roles are the objective-expressive (content), the face-adjustment (ethical appeal), the audience, and the logical. For our purposes here, we are interested most in the face-adjustment and the audience roles. Yoos claims that the writer adjusts her writing (or should we say "face") to the appropriate audience, trying to establish what needs to be said, how much more needs to be said, and what ought or ought not to be said. The audience role, as we discussed earlier, is a concern for meaning, content, readability, style, and tone (Yoos 247). Of course, like Brooke, Yoos does not mention physically role-playing the parts of audience and writer/speaker. However, I believe his roles can be interpreted as such and used in the classroom to combine physical and noetic delivery in order to reinforce students' audience awareness.

In addition, language plays an important part in constructing the aforementioned roles because, as Brian Watkins states, it is the overriding regulator of the "life drama." Watkins quotes James Britton's two uses of language: first, the language we use in reaction to ongoing events, the participant form; and second, the language use that arises from recollection or in premeditation of events, the spectator form. Participant language is employed to organize our behavior, to regulate both our individual and our cooperative activities. Spectator language is utilized to refer to, report on, and interpret action rather than act as a substitute. This speech form allows us to shape our experiences and to share with others whose reception verifies our understanding. Furthermore, the spectator is unburdened with the responsibility for immediate response to a situation and can evaluate more broadly, better able to arrive at an understanding of who and what we are. Therefore, being involved in the dramatic activity is performing the spectator role (Watkins 37). Taken a step further, through delivery of ideas, students with spectator language "refer to, report on and interpret action" that is (to be) their written communication. Then, in reaction to this delivery, peers can help organize writing behavior with participant language. This give and take may even blur during the perform-ance of ideas, with spectators and participants crossing lines in the drama. Most important, delivery becomes the communication of ideas through physical and noetic means.

Thus far, my discussion has been limited to those theorists who have theorized about rhetoric and drama, but have not focused on physical delivery. However, there are those who have critiqued noetic delivery and have argued for a more physical delivery through performance in the writing class. In fact, James Moffett's discussion of drama and writing expands on Britton's spectator language. In his *Drama: What is Happening*, Moffett makes a distinction between what the spectator sees in stage drama and in street drama. He believes that a spectator who goes to a theater sees stage drama, but that same person could go out to the street and note the sensations he feels while witnessing some action and then write a script of his own. To Moffett "drama is any raw phenomena as they are first being converted to information by some observer" (1). The spectator is involved in drama constantly through life experience. Moffett states that drama is the matrix of discourse:

> As information, it is the inner speech of the observer at the moment of coding raw phenomena. The corresponding education activity is recording. As communication, it is the social speech of the participant at the moment of vocalizing face to face. The corresponding educational activity is oral extem-porizing. Soliloquy is intrapersonal dialogue, which is verbal thought. Con-versation is interpersonal dialogue, which is vocal speech. These two activities feel each other: when we communicate we internalize conversation that will influence how we code information in soliloquy; how we inform ourselves in soliloquy will influence what we communicate in conversation. (25)

Thus, we see yet again the use of the dialogue metaphor. Here, Moffett expands that metaphor to include soliloquy and monologue, which he claims we experience in our everyday lives. The soliloquy is a colloquy among a person's cultural, social, and familial voices. All the intricate relations between thought and speech, mind and society, heredity and environment are involved. As we experience our daily lives, we are constantly soliloquizing at some level of abstraction, depending on where our attention is centered at the moment. According to Moffett, "speaking and writing are essentially just editing and abstracting some version of what at some moment one is thinking" (10).

Dialogue is the next step in Moffett's model. Dialogue is extemporized and feedback is fast, clearing up or aggravating misunderstandings. He believes a unique quality of dialogue is that the speakers build on each other's sentence constructions: "[a] conversation is verbal collaboration" (*Drama* 11). Accompanying this verbal collaboration is cognitive collaboration. Moffett states that a conversation is "dia-logical," a meeting and fusion of minds, even if speakers disagree.

Moffett's third step, the monologue, is the sustained, connected speech of one person. It is the bridge from drama to other forms of discourse. The monologue moves closer to organization and composition because some single mind is developing the subject. As he claims, it is the external pathway to writing but also has some dialogue for its context from which it issues (*Drama* 21). Monologue is the result of dialogue and soliloquy; a writer draws on discourse she has heard, had, and read, then composes a permutation of what the world has given her (24). Hence, Moffett's writing theories are taken directly from the theater; he believes our lives are drama and our writing from those life experiences can result in dialogues, monologues, and soliloquies. Moffett's terminology sets up a bridge between writing and the theater. If taken further, we can utilize these elements in order to dramatize writing through delivery. Dialogues, monologues, and soliloquies can become just that in the writing class when students deliver their ideas to their peers through physical and noetic elements.

When discussing drama in the light of delivery in writing classes, teachers can use dramatic techniques to help students reveal or discover what they want to say, just as through Moffett's dialogues, monologues, and soliloquies. Dorothy Heathcote, pioneer in the application of theater techniques and play in the classroom, lists six elements of drama that I believe writing teachers may utilize:

Sound—all that which can be heard, from voices to thunder.
Silence, in contrast, so that it makes its impact.
Movement, all types from a single gesture to that of massed crowds.

The contrast of the meaningful stillness of individuals and groups.
That which is not seen as in darkness, or absence while we wait.
All the most brilliant light which leaves nothing to shadowy form, and either
cruelly or kindly allows us to perceive each and every person and thing before
us. (32)

Implementing these six elements in a classroom can encourage students
to perform their life experiences. Most significant, some theorists and
teachers have already attempted to implement parts of these elements.
For instance, expressionistic teachers and theorists routinely pay attention to classroom setting, sound, and movement, like Robert Zoellner,
who advocates a type of art studio for a writing classroom. In a second
example, feminist approaches to writing prevalently talk about silence or
listening as a detriment, that writers, especially women, need a voice, a
sound in order to be heard, something that can be achieved through
physical and noetic delivery.

In the late 1960s, several theorists argued that successful writing should
be analyzed in terms of its sequence of observable behavior. Building on such
models, Zoellner took these ideas one step further, making the "observable
behavior" into a physical performance. As early as 1969, he wanted classroom models to change from the "think–write" metaphor to a "talk–write"
metaphor. He claims that the think–write metaphor contends that the
written word is thought on paper; it equates the act of thought with the act
of writing in the sense that the scribal stream symbolizes both vocal utterance and the thought that it generates (269). He contends that the
think–write model directs the attention of the teacher and the students to
the product and not to the characteristics of the scribal act. Instead, he
wants teachers to shift their attention to that which is observable and
manipulatable. To that end, he cites the psychologist B. F. Skinner's model
of operant behavior and behavior modification as grounds for his talk–write
model. He believes that Skinner's theories should be applied to the writing
classroom:

> It shifts the locus of methodological attention from the *inner* activity of the
> organism, which is invisible and empirically inaccessible, to the *outer* activity
> of the organism, which is visible and empirically observable. It does not
> necessarily deny the existence of thought or various other kinds of inner
> states; it simply faces the fact that the interior life of the organism is *beyond
> our effective reach.* Consequently it directs its efforts, not to the establishment
> of right *thinking,* but rather of right *behaving.* (289)

Thus, to apply this theory, Zoellner claims that teachers must get their students to vocalize what they are in the process of writing, a verbal communication that can be modified as the students progress through the writing. Therefore, he suggests having large chalkboards and artists' easels in the classroom where the students can write in groups, getting immediate feedback on what they are creating (296–97). This art studio look is intended because, as Zoellner states, "words are in many ways as plastic and artistic a medium as paint or clay, and the talk-write classroom should reflect this fact" (299). The classroom is designed for many types of dialogue, including that between teacher and entire class. Zoellner also carries this theory over to the teacher's office as well. He suggests that during conferences, the teacher have a large chalkboard next to the desk for students to use when they are having difficulty putting together the words for their assignment.

Robert Ochsner also argues against what Zoellner calls think-write. In his *Physical Eloquence and the Biology of Writing*, Ochsner states that teachers must de-emphasize writing as a thinking process because the "effort de-humanizes them" and "alienates them from their own language" (29). He goes on to quote Alfred North Whitehead (1929): "Allow that your students have bodies" because without the body, there can be no writing (2). Unfortunately, Ochsner argues, our current teaching practices endorse a cognitive and social attitude toward writing that fundamentally denatures a learner's body, as if writing is entirely a mental, self-conscious effort (6). Robert Brooke believes that compared to the ancients, modern students barely practice the physical act of writing. In our writing classrooms, the students' bodies are twice displaced: once removed from oral to written form and further disembodied because printed words exist in stasis (27). Ochsner asks, what unnatural act does writing invite to a classroom full of chattering students (28)? The answer, of course, is silence and stillness. Learning needs to be a lively conversation full of spontaneity. Instead, in the writing classroom, we have a graveyard full of dead bodies. Through the mind-only emphasis, the students become disembodied writers, with only the brain and the fingers working, whereas the rest of their bodies function as a telephone pole, supporting good connections and keeping the bad ones safe, presumably not dangling somewhere (35). Therefore, to reintroduce the body to writing is "to make prose talk" (28).

As a model to build his physical eloquence on, Ochsner uses Cicero's five canons of rhetoric, invention, arrangement, style, memory, and delivery. However, he reverses the order of the five so that delivery is first and so on. He claims that when beginning their writing, students simply "deliver" ideas straight from their subconscious onto the paper; delivery is the physiology of producing a text. The definition of memory becomes the subconscious recall of all language, the storage place from which words are chosen and then placed into grammatical sequence. Style changes to the classification of basic linguistic features that correspond to stages of writing development. Arrangement and invention retain their original definitions, but now they simply come as the last two steps of text production (5). Thus, for Ochsner, in writing theory, delivery becomes a physical performance of ideas recalled through memory, classified through style, arranged and invented. Only through performance by the entire body can the writing be conveyed to an audience, thus completing the whole theory of writing.

By its very nature, performance incorporates or blends the physical and noetic processes of delivery, and as we have seen, performance can be a valuable tool in the writing classroom. With theories from theater and theories such as Zoellner's talk–write model and Burke's *dramatism*, students perform their ideas for an audience who gives immediate reaction. Unfortunately, although many writing teachers utilize some performance, the use has been mostly restricted to invention purposes. Even so, we can incorporate performance into a re-visioned theory of delivery, one that reunites the physical and the noetic and, thus, employs a strategy that has been underused in the classroom.

WRITING THE BODY

So far, I have kept my discussion to those practices that have currently been in use, at least somewhat, in writing classrooms. Almost all teaching manuals have espoused some form of collaboration and audience awareness, whereas fewer texts have theories on performance in the writing class. However, I now want to turn to a theory that has received little exposure in the writing classroom. Postmodern French feminists coined the phrase *writing the body* in an attempt to find a new language for themselves, something not encumbered by the phallocentricism of male-dominated White Western society. What began as a theory that attempted to focus on women's bodies in writing was soon taken up by other postmodern theorists such as Roland Barthes and Trinh T. Minh-ha, who went on to incorporate theories on the physical use of the body in speaking and writing. I believe theories of writing the body, and a call for authors to abandon the silence and stillness of writing are the epitome of physical delivery. By writing the body, the physical can be rejoined with the more noetic delivery of traditional writing.

Generally, writing the body has been advocated for freeing an oppressed group of people—women. If we consider that, traditionally, *student* implies, by definition, a lack of power in school settings, then students as a group can also be considered oppressed. Thus, in theory, students should be able to use writing the body as a way to free themselves in the classroom. Therefore, by incorporating and expanding parts of this theory, I plan to adapt it for all students, male and female, in an effort to help reinstate delivery into the writing classroom. First, though, we need to review the applicable literature on writing the body. Hence, I have included here a survey of postmodern literary theorists who have advocated some form of writing the body.

In "The Laugh of the Medusa," Helene Cixous describes how a woman speaks in public:

> She doesn't "speak," she throws her trembling body forward; she lets go of herself, she flies; all of her passes into her voice, and it's with her body that she vitally supports the "logic" of her speech. Her flesh speaks true. She lays herself bare. In fact, she physically materializes what she's thinking; she signifies it with her body. In a certain way she *inscribes* what she's saying, because she doesn't deny her drives the intractable and impassioned part they have in speaking. (251)

In contrast, Cixous states that men make a division between oral speech and the logic of the text. Thus, they use only the tiniest part of their body, their lips. She believes that women should use the same force and the same passion in their writing as exhibited in speech. Cixous addresses women in the following manner: "write your self. Your body must be heard. Censor the body and you censor breath and speech at the same time" (250).

I realize, of course, that Cixous is fighting against the silence that a male-dominated society and language have imposed on women—that she is advocating more discussion of the female body in general in writing. However, in addition, she is advocating women breaking their silence and speaking in public: "It is time for women to start scoring their feats in written and oral language" (251). My contention is that students, also, have been silenced too long by our education system, and they, too, need to score "their feats in written and oral language." They, too, need to incorporate their bodies fully into their writing.

Likewise, feminist critic Trinh T. Minh-ha believes that "we do not *have* bodies, we are *our* bodies" (36). Although she, like Cixous, is expressly thinking about women needing to break from a male-dominated language, we can include our students in her approach to writing. She states:

> We write—think and feel—(with) our entire bodies rather than only (with) our minds or hearts. It is a perversion to consider thought the product of one specialized organ, the brain, and feeling, that of the heart.... [T]hought is as much a product of the eye, the finger, or the foot as it is of the brain. (36, 39)

If thought is from the whole body, then why have we, in the writing class, divided it from the rest of the body? As I quoted Ochsner in the performance section, we must allow that our students have bodies and to reincorporate the physical side of writing.

Similarly, Roland Barthes believes that the "book" should be analogous to the "conversation" because bodies are involved in an *entre nous* situation. "Put the body back where it has been taken from" (335). In his *The Pleasure of the Text,* he bemoans the fact that guidelines for performing discourse in classical times have since been censored. He calls upon writers to reinstitute the *actio,* a group of formulae designed to allow for the corporeal exteriorization of discourse. *Actio,* Cicero's word for delivery, is the embodiment, shall we say, of internal thought/expression/emotion; as Barthes writes, "it dealt with a theater of expression, the actor–orator 'expressing' his indignation, his compassion, etc." (66). Thus, this delivery, "writing aloud" Barthes names it, should be reinvested into our process of writing because the body, too, carries expression in its physicality. Barthes states:

> *Writing aloud*...is carried...by the *grain* of the voice, which is an erotic mixture of timbre and language, and can therefore also be, along with diction, the substance of an art: the art of guiding one's body.... [W]hat it searches for (in a perspective of bliss) are the pulsional incidents, the language line with flesh, a text where we can hear the grain of the throat, the patine of consonants, the voluptuousness of vowels, a whole carnal stereophony: the articulation of the body.... (66)

Barthes describes writing with the body as an art, something that is expressive in movement. It is not simply a pen and paper, a mind and a hand, but a whole, acting in unison to create a meaning. As feminist critic Ann Rosalind Jones states, "to write from the body is to recreate the world" (91), and for students to utilize more physicality in their writing may bring about a fuller development of their message. That is the goal;

by reinstating delivery in the classroom, we will have a whole theory of writing.

DELIVERY RE-VISIONED

Thus far, I have made a great list of theories—collaboration and audience, drama and performance, and writing the body—from seemingly disparate areas: composition, theater, and feminist studies. Nevertheless, these areas are not as dissimilar as they may seem on the surface; they all address the topic of human communication in some form. In the writing classroom, clear communication should be the ultimate goal for our students. My contention is that a re-visioned delivery can incorporate all of the aforementioned theories and ideas, and more, in order to aid the students in their struggle to communicate. Delivery reinstates a physicality to writing classrooms that had been missing, or minimalized, since the turn of the century. In fact, by reinstating delivery, we can rejoin Cicero's five canons, once again forming the whole needed for a well-rounded theory of writing. For further historical basis, we can turn to Quintilian, where we see for the first time a connection between all four communication skills: reading, writing, speaking, and listening. He believed that the four skills were so "inseparably linked" that if people should confine themselves to any one of these activities, then the other three would suffer (*Institutio Oratoria* X.1.1). "And I know not whether both exercises, when we perform them with care and assiduity, are not reciprocally beneficial, as it appears that by writing we speak with greater accuracy, and by speaking we write with greater ease" (*Institutio*, X.7.28–29). Even closer to our era is Moffett's simple admonition: "People learn better ...if speaking, listening, and writing are closely interwoven" (*Active Voice* 74).

Therefore, I want to redefine delivery in terms of Cicero's whole canon, incorporating current theories of writing: *Delivery in the writing classroom is the use of noetic and physical processes by which students can convey their ideas/life experiences to their peer audiences in an effort to develop the best writing they can achieve.* What does this mean and how can it be applied? The following is an explanation of my definition.

With the inclusion of the phrase " *use of noetic and physical processes,*" I have employed the continuum set up in chapter 1, Cicero's definition of purely physical movement and sound, and Bacon's notion that physical movement is inspired by the mental act of speaking. The idea of reuniting the noetic and the physical also comes from theories on speaking and writing, which as stated before are the crossroads of the mental and physical. They are important halves of delivery. Thus, to reestablish the whole theory of delivery, we must have our students rejoin the noetic-thinking process with either physical gestures or speaking so that writing becomes a performance and more than simply moving a hand across paper (or typing at a keyboard). Dialogue theories also impact the noetic and physical processes because they allow for a two-way communication to be established through writing and its performance. Theories on performance enhance the noetic and physical because, by its very nature, performance calls on the physical use of the body in communicating to an audience. Finally, writing the body, throwing the whole self into the effort of writing, can bring back a new "aliveness" to the writing class-room and, thus, to the students' writing itself.

I incorporated the phrase *"convey their ideas/life experiences to their peer audiences"* because, when writing, students need to draw on their own ideas and life experiences, even in doing a research essay. In an attempt to convey those ideas to their peer audience, students need to utilize more than just simply the paper they have written on. They need to speak to their audience, discover what that audience wants and needs to understand the students' ideas. The students and the audience must converse, get to know each other, which cannot be done simply by handing someone a sheet of paper with some squiggles on it. A dialogue must be established, a collaboration between the author and the audi-ence, in order for the successful completion of the writing process. Thus, here again, theories of speaking and writing have informed this notion, as students must use oral communication with an audience in order to anticipate the audience needs. Dialogue, of course, is the essence of that communication of writer or speaker in collaboration with audience. Through performance (i.e., playing roles, reciting monologues, and so on), students physically share their concepts with their peers. Lastly, with writing the body, students abandon the silence of the classroom while exteriorizing their ideas and experiences for their peers.

In our contemporary writing classes, there are voices at times, but as I have stated before, this classroom is still mainly silent, with only minds and hands at work. With re-visioned delivery, the classroom will no longer be silent but a great deal more active and boisterous because teachers can make assignments that will incorporate delivery throughout the writing process, for instance, debates for prewriting, work at easels for writing, and reading aloud for revision.

CONCLUSION

At the turn of the century, delivery was abandoned by composition classes and students were left with half a theory to guide their attempts at writing. Over the years, theorists have given us discussions of speaking and writing, and dialogue, all directing writing teachers in an effort to aid struggling students. However, until recently, theorists continued to ignore or minimalize delivery, leaving the rhetorical canon—and writing theory—split apart. The rhetorical act suffers if we fragment the whole. Therefore, in order to have a complete process of writing, delivery needs to be reinstated as an integral step alongside invention, arrangement, style, and memory. By integrating our current writing theories with performance and writing the body, areas thus far overlooked in many contemporary writing theories, we can put delivery back into composition, restoring the whole rhetorical act.

Because we now have a theory of delivery that underpins classroom activity, how can teachers go about implementing this theory? This is the main objective of chapter 3, the application of re-visioned delivery made easy.

3

Dramatizing Writing

For three chapters, I have sung the praises of delivery and made a case for its reinstatement in the writing classroom. Delivery, combining the noetic and physical processes of students in order to convey their ideas, should be an essential part of writing theory and practice. As teachers, we cannot insist on improved writing skills through mind development only, continuing to ignore that our students have bodies. We must not continue to minimalize delivery or to separate it from the rest of the rhetorical canon. Therefore, in order to more fully reestablish delivery in the classroom, I suggest that we teach our students to dramatize their writing.

David Booth, author on drama and education, states that drama is the "I in the story." When students perform their writing, they have an opportunity to work inside the topic, connecting their own emotions, experiences, and values with the situations and issues, the material of their writing (Swartz 8). Not only do they connect with the topics, but the students also learn about their audience. Using drama as an application for delivery institutes a two-way communication in which writers and audiences learn from one another through speaking and writing.

When they make assignments, teachers should help students become more aware of their written speaking voices and help them understand the importance of addressing an audience. As John Hagaman states, "Power exists in the spoken voice, and a sense of voice in prose often commands attention" (191). Therefore, because speech often assumes power because of the immediacy of an audience and speaker, teachers should create assignments that provide students with live audiences, such as having them write dialogues to one another or to different groups within the class.

To that end, this chapter is an accumulation of exercises and lesson plans that actually implement my theory of delivery through drama or performance of some type. First, I have listed approaches, ideas, and activities that teachers may use in their classes to reinstate delivery. Next, in order to suggest ways of sequencing a series of related speaking, writing, and listening activities into a curricular approach, I have outlined James Moffett's strategies from his book *Active Voices*. Although he does not connect his practices with theories of delivery or classical rhetoric, I found that his work contains what I consider to be an implementation of my delivery theory. I conclude the chapter with two entire lesson plans from beginning to completed essay in an effort to show how teachers can reincorporate delivery for two types of writing commonly used in first-year college courses. These two lesson plans deal largely with the issue of audience awareness, one being geared toward narrative writing and the second toward expository.

ACTIVITIES TO REINSTATE DELIVERY

The following activities are divided according to the type of physicality or performance involved: Dramatizing Voice Alone, Dramatizing Body Alone, and Full Physical Performance. Of course, these divisions are fairly arbitrary; at times, the activity is not entirely only voice alone or body alone. In fact, how could a person use the voice and not use the body? To make these arbitrary divisions (at least for dramatizing voice alone and dramatizing body alone), I attempted to classify the activity according to which physicality is more dominant in the activity, speech or body movement. When both voice and movement are more equally represented, then the activity is classified as full physical performance.

With each activity, I have included an explanation of how a teacher can utilize it during any step of the writing process.[1] In this manner, teachers

---

[1] Almost all of the activities listed here are to be done in groups. However, I do not want to spend time explaining how successful groups work, but I will include five guidelines to go by (with help from Rubin and Dodd 11–12, 14):

1. Establish early on a receptive atmosphere that will allow students to be both encouraging and respectful of each other.
2. Try to mix personality types in each group. For instance, do not put all very vocal students in one group and all the quiet ones in another.
3. With the students' assistance, devise a checklist of acceptable and unacceptable group behaviors.
4. Videotape, if possible, students working in groups. In a positive manner, single out behaviors (not students) to be reinforced and those to be squelched.
5. Model the activity with one or two of the more vocal students. This will help to allay insecurities in other students.

For more information on how groups work see *Writing Groups: History, Theory and Implications* by Anne Ruggles Gere. For more direction in how to implement groups in the classroom, see Robert Brooke, Ruth Mirtz and Rick Evans' *Small Groups in Writing Workshops: Invitation to a Writer's Life*.

may choose the activity that is best suited for the area the class is working on. I have gathered these activities from several sources: drama books, theater directors' guides, writing teachers' studies, composition theory, and from university colleagues. For each activity, I have acknowledged the source.

Dramatizing Voice Alone

Every little bit helps when increasing the use of the body in our writing, and both teacher and student can dramatize writing simply through adding voice to the written word. Voice activities come to us from various sources but predominately from composition theory. Such critics as David Bartholomae, Peter Elbow, and Jeffrey Sommers suggest activities as simple as reading aloud to group sessions giving detailed feedback orally to writers and speakers. One thing that all the activities have in common is the use of delivery through voice.

> **Activity:** Have the students read their writing aloud either to you in conference or in groups during any step of the writing process.

A student who reads aloud can provide what David Bartholomae calls "an oral reconstruction of their written text" (324). When the student's writing ability is hindered, this oral script can give the teacher the student's "intended" text. The teachers should put more emphasis on listening rather than talking to students. Students should talk out their concerns about their essays while the teacher helps them to articulate problems and tentative solutions to those problems. An additional method here would be to tape record the conference and make the tape available to the students.

> **Activity** (Radcliffe 190): Divide students into pairs. Working one at a time, each student speaks for thirty minutes into a tape recorder with the help of the other student, who reinforces the speaking by asking questions when necessary. The student then selects material from the taped session to include in an essay.

Here, students talk through ideas for essays, doing their prewriting verbally and transferring their thoughts straight onto tape with the help of an audience. Each student then has a tape of what was "written" during the session and can refer back to that tape for material to use in an essay. Thus, we have delivery aiding in invention.

> **Activity** (Hagaman 190): Pair students and ask them to discuss an assigned article. Record their conversations, have students transcribe the recordings, and refer to the transcriptions as aids to composing their own essays.

This is similar to the previous activity except with this exercise, students discuss an article that should provoke debate on the issue it tackles. From this deliberation, students can gain insights from each other, perhaps even be swayed to other views of the issue. Then, the students may utilize the transcripts for their own prewriting efforts. In addition, while students are in the midst of writing, if they are stumped by one section, or have questions, many times they can refer back to the taped discussion for more ideas on where to go with their essay.

> **Activity:** Before students hand in drafts of essays, they make a tape recording of their own comments and questions for the teacher. In reply to that recording, the teacher makes comments on the same tape instead of writing the comments.

Jeffrey Sommers claims that tape-recorded commentary on student essays can be a verbal asset for both the teacher and student because it allows for both voices to be heard (49). Sommers advocates only the teacher using the tape recorder. However, I believe the technique is viable for both the teacher and student on any draft of an essay, from beginning to final. The student buys a cassette for the semester and, for each essay, makes comments about her writing and what areas she wants the teacher to specifically look at. After listening to the student voice, the teacher reads the essay and responds next to the student's comments. According to Sommers, this technique is superior to written comments for two reasons. First, the comments are more understandable to the student (and the student's to the teacher). The recorder allows the teacher to make more thorough comments more clearly in a more detailed fashion in a relatively short period of time. If teachers normally spend 20 to 40 minutes per essay making written comments (Nancy Sommers), then a tape-recorded comment can say much more in a shorter period (Jeffrey Sommers 51). Recorded responses also permit "instructors to explain important issues in the students' work, teach them about the writing process, and review concepts already covered in class" (52). Second, tape-recorded responses encourage individualized instruction in a personalized voice. As Sommers explains, "Where once the students read abbreviations scrawled in the margins of the draft, now they hear a 'human voice'" (52). Inflection can be used both to generate enthusiasm for revision and also to soften criticism; thus, praise sounds genuine and criticism becomes more tactful. With such vocal feedback, the teacher also becomes a role model for the students to emulate in peer editing groups as well as in conferencing.

> **Activity** (Halpern 355): Tape-record a speech, then with students analyze the sentence structure and try reorganizing it in an order appropriate to writing.

This activity is an extension of Sommers', whereby the teacher can use a tape recording on both an individual or a class basis. Jeanne Halpern claims that any taped discourse is likely to provide examples and to offer opportunities to discuss possible reordering strategies. The students get a chance to hear themselves and to hear their spoken language. They then attempt to approximate that speech into a written form. Hence, the students learn to differentiate between spoken and written discourse through a form of delivery.

> **Activity** (Halpern 354): Have students prepare their texts for reading by others in class or out of class. In groups, have the students exchange essays and have each member in turn read aloud the essay of another member.

To prepare students to write for others, we must have them closely observe the structural characteristics of finished texts. Then, they can work on their own format and practice those features of successful written texts that are likely to cause problems for them. This work should include other students reading the texts and giving input on the essay during the entire writing process.

Likewise, Peter Elbow believes that to be a better writer takes interaction between people, giving the writer an audience. Two heads, or more, can make conflicting material interact better than only the writer alone. In talking out the essay, the process is give and take, providing "a continual leverage or mechanical advantage: we successively climb upon the shoulders of the other's restructuring, so that at each climbing up, we can see a little farther" (*Without Teachers* 30). He believes that reading aloud not only performs the essay for the audience, but in doing so, the author can spot things that would not otherwise be seen. Hearing one's own words is the vicarious experience of being someone else, a part of the audience per se. For Elbow, reading aloud stresses what is most important: "writing is really a voice spread out over time, not marks spread out in space. The audience can't experience them all at once as they can a picture; they can only hear one instant at a time as with music. And there must be a voice in it" (82).

A fear of audience can also be revealed through reading aloud. The nervousness a writer feels when performing the essay is part of the problem in writing. Elbow believes that even if the writer does not feel nervous when writing, that could mean that she has simply separated the experience of audience from the experience of writing. However, that fear of audience may still affect writers somehow, perhaps by tying their tongues and clouding their minds when they sit down to write, or by closing off certain types of writing. "Reading out loud brings the sense of audience back into [the author's] act of writing. This is a great source of power. Getting a sense of audience isn't just practice in feeling scared about how they might react. It also means learning how they *do* react" (83).

Robert Ochsner agrees that reading aloud can train a student to hear the qualities of effective writing: "reading aloud gives back to written language the body it has vaporized" (148). He claims that in silent reading, we only use a single prose channel of expression, which is visual print. On the other hand, in oral reading, we add a speech channel (auditory) that brings with it a physiological awareness of breaks that correspond to the pauses for breathing. "Reading aloud furthers the acquisition of prose by helping students to hear what they may not see.... [T]he oral performance highlights in sound what a printed text may not clearly emphasize" (149). In other words, "style comes alive when students literally breathe into a text their performance options" (152).

Elbow goes on to explain four strategies that an audience can use when reacting to a writer's performance: pointing, summarizing, telling, and showing. In *pointing*, the audience simply points out both important and vague words in the text. Pointing makes the audience listen to the essay very carefully and shows the writer what words elicit the strongest and weakest reactions (85).

Summarizing is a four-part description of what is in the essay. First, the audience very quickly tells the author what the main points, main feelings, or centers of gravity are that they heard in the text. The audience then chooses a sentence or two describing, in their own words, the main point of the essay. Next, they select one word from the essay that best summarizes it. Last, the audience chooses a summary word that is not in the essay. The group works informally and quickly through these steps, not planning or thinking too much about it. The point for summarizing is to show the writer what topics from the essay immediately stand out to the audience (86).

Elbow's third strategy, *telling*, has the audience simply tell the writer everything that happened in them as they listened to the words. This is usually told in story form: first this happened, then this. One way to think of this method is for the audience members to pretend they are hooked up to medical instruments that check pulse, blood pressure, EEG, and so forth. The group tells the writer what the machine readouts say: "How did you feel when you read each part of the essay?" (87, 90).

Showing, the final strategy, gives an illustration of the audience's response to the writing. Here, they try to describe feelings, impressions, and images that are often too vague for a clear definition. The group can describe the picture they see, refer to poems, music, animals, colors, and so on. They can also give suggestions for changes. This can sometimes give clues to the writer on why sections in an essay do or do not work (90).

Above all, Elbow stresses the fact that a writing class should not be "comfy." Instead, such a classroom should be a place where the writers and audience must put their own responses out on the table, offer up their "own reactions as pure data—not defend or justify or even discuss them—just reveal them and let the other person use them for his own private purposes" (140).

> **Activity** (Halpern 355): Begin with a spoken narrative in which tenses switch often. Have students rewrite the passage using a single tense. This may be performed in groups, as a class, or by individuals.

In such an exercise, students gain insight into the process of improving consistency in tense in written texts. Also, through the spoken text, they hear the language and can more easily pick out the mistakes in tense. This activity may be used at any time during the writing process as a grammar exercise.

> **Activity** (Personal communication with Steve Mohr on March 17, 1992): Compose as a class. On an overhead projector or on the chalkboard, the teacher and students begin talking aloud about a topic and translate that ongoing conversation into a rough draft, jointly authored. This collaboration can also be accomplished in smaller groups, having them compose through ongoing conversations.

As with the other activities of this section on voice, the exercise reflects speaking as an aid to writing. Through the verbal delivery of thought, the students can see and hear the writing process at work. Moreover, by performing the exercise as a class, the teacher models composing behavior for the students. They get to see that even professionals need help with their writing, and they feel good about contributing to a group effort. Here, both the teacher and the students are delivering the essay as a group.

> **Activity** (Personal communication with Connie Vivrett on February 15, 1992): Students and teacher read two short articles aloud. As a group, discuss the articles, choose a topic from them, compose a thesis, arguments, reasons, and so on, and finally the essay itself.

Along with all the benefits listed for the previous activity, we add the practice of reading aloud, which can also improve the students' speaking voices and listening skills.

Activity (Vivrett): Divide the class into two, students choosing the side of an issue that they wish to be on. After about ten minutes to gather arguments, a free form debate takes place, lasting as long as energy and interest survives. Then, the class debates who won the original debate, who used clearer arguments, best logic, and so forth.

So often in writing classes, teachers utilize the debate format that helps students understand arguments, counterarguments, and strategies they can later use in their essays. The activity just mentioned not only utilizes that original format, but also makes the students think about the debate in terms of whose arguments were stronger and more logical, who used better, fuller examples, more concrete details, and appealed well to the audience—all traits needed for a successful written argument.

Activity (Rubin and Dodd 43): Divide the class into two groups or teams and debate a question on some issue or situation. Before being allowed to add personal comments, each student must identify the type of argument used by the preceding student speaker from the other team, and the role within the debate of that speaker (see Appendix C for descriptions). Midway through the class period, the two groups switch sides (argumentatively and physically) and take on the point of view they had previously opposed. Writing of argumentative essays follows.

As with the preceding activity, this one also makes use of the debate format in aiding students to see two sides of an issue. At the same time, they need to be made aware that it is not enough simply to have an opinion, but that support and reasoning are crucial in argumentative writing. For this assignment, teachers need to keep in mind that students may require time to research an issue if they are going to give an effective argument. The more complex the issue, the more time they will need. Following the debate, teachers may want to have students freewrite to clear up their ideas and put them into some perspective. Later, they can write a more extensive essay using all the information obtained for the debate plus the insights discovered by looking at the issue from other students' viewpoints.

The voice, speaking aloud, is just a small part of delivery in the classroom. It is a beginning, yes, and it can be a powerful instrument in adding depth to student essays. Voice can break the silence that has held our writing classrooms in a traditional stranglehold for so long, but voice is just the first step in delivery.

Dramatizing Body Alone

Dramatizing with the body alone is the next step to bringing delivery back to the writing classroom. In this section, I have included activities that utilize only the body, not voice, in aiding students with their writing. These activities start as simply as stretching tight muscles, but continue with more full body involvement, such as mime. Here, there are more influences from the theater, performance that uses only the body to express ideas.

> **Activity:** Have the students perform simple stretching exercises before any writing begins. These should include not only full body stretches, but also hand and eyes. Any student that hits a block to thinking during writing should also move around, walk, stretch to get the blood flowing quicker to the brain.

For years, doctors have emphasized that people need to stretch in order to warm up before exercising. It not only helps to loosen up the muscles to prepare them for more strenuous activity, but can also be part of the overall reduction of stress. Likewise, writers need to warm up before their more "strenuous workout," and stretching the body physically can aid in stretching the mind. It is always good for students, or any writers, to get up and walk around before and during the writing process. Also, it is helpful to stretch the fingers, hands, eyes, and neck because these are regions that get more of a workout during the physical act of writing.

> **Activity** (Neelands 61): Have students develop a pose or gesture that they think represents or symbolizes most appropriately the topic they are working on. They can perform such a task individually or in a group, forming still pictures of a concept or a person's characteristic(s).

In order to see what the students are thinking, a teacher can use concretized thought, or tableaux, which can be best described as playing statues. Tableaux are useful for introducing the idea of images and focusing the students' attention on a particular aspect of the topic. It paves the way to deciphering those images. Tableaux can reveal the specific in the general so that the specific may become part of the students' writing later. This practice also encourages selectivity and economy of expression while developing symbolic thought and awareness of spatial representation. By stopping the action, tableaux give time for the students to reflect on the topic and encourage discussion about meanings behind the action. For instance, if the issue the class is addressing is racism, groups may define the specific by making or forming a picture of the riots in Los Angeles in April, 1992. The picture of people looting a store depicts a different specific from a picture of people helping others away from the riot. Tableaux can become a way of showing change: "How we were and how we are now" (Morgan and Saxton 110). This activity is especially successful during the prewriting stages of the essay. The tableaux can give students ideas on what to write and how to approach the topic. Furthermore, it can sharpen students' insights into people's opposing views on issues.

> Activity (Hogg 14): Each student must choose an emotion to mime. This is accomplished with the use of the body, through gestures, facial expressions, movement, kinesics. Have the other students identify and talk about the emotions described.

Mime, the use of movement to narrate or describe, can range from the classic form capturing the essence of a person or action to the imitative form reproducing an action realistically and in detail (McCaslin 61). Movement, the basis of play, ritual, games, dance and theatre, is a natural beginning for work in creating a student's "story." With the use of the body, the muscles are stretched and relaxed; posture and coordination improve for the exercise. According to McCaslin, students of all ages and backgrounds may find it easier to become involved through movement instead of through verbalization (69). Mime frees the students from having to think of dialogue and if the entire class works at the same time, self-consciousness disappears and involvement is encouraged (71). Mime activities can be employed throughout the writing process. It can give students topic ideas, different viewpoints, and insights on how people act, any of which can be used during prewriting, writing and revision.

> Activity (Hogg 14): Mime the daily routine of a person. Have the other students write their impressions.

Having students interpret the routines of other people can give them new insight into those people, their motivations, and their thoughts as well as take their audience into account. They must decide what is important to the audience and how they can describe it nonverbally. Moreover, by watching the mime and reporting on it, students can strengthen their observation skills.

> Activity (Knabe 45): Improvise family situations in which students assume various roles at the dinner table. Ask each person at the table to express a variety of feelings in a nonverbal way. How might the father react to indicate his disapproval of a child's behavior? How might the mother come to the child's

defense? How might the child react? Have the students write their impressions of the mime they watched and also their impressions of their own miming.

This activity is particularly well suited to preparing students to write narratives, especially anything reflective. Often, students can only describe a person physically or in vague, general ways. Therefore, this practice forces the students to look beyond the surface and the words to describe someone close to them. A teacher may find that this exercise works well when introducing the narrative, but it may also be used during the intermediate writing phase to give students more depth to their writing.

> **Activity** (Knabe 45): Ask students to observe with care another person watching a performance of some kind (television show, play, lecture, concert, etc.) to determine the nonverbal reactions of that individual. Have the students reproduce them in mime for the class to see if other students can guess what kind of performance is being observed and what the overall feeling is on the part of the observer. Have them write their observations in detail and share them with the class.

This activity aids in developing the students' observation skills at two levels. First, the students must watch another person and then mime him or her. Second, during the mime, the class must make conjectures while observing again. This further aids in teaching them the importance of detail.

Employing the body alone in writing can give a definite physicality to the process. At the very least, we have gone beyond having the students simply use their minds and their hands to write. With activities such as mime and even just stretching, the classroom has movement and life to it, but with only the use of the body, we still are faced with the silence we had broken with the voice only. We need to combine these two in order to capture the full benefits of delivery for our students.

Full Physical Performance

Each of the previous two sections, in which we added either voice alone or body alone, were only the beginnings of reintegrating delivery to the classroom. As I stated earlier, every little bit helps because even the least bit of physical involvement aids in reinstating delivery in the classroom. However, delivery deserves to be an equal with the other members of the rhetorical canon. We cannot write effectively without all steps in the process—invention, arrangement, style, memory, *and delivery*. If we delete, or even slight, any one of these steps, then we have damaged the whole rhetorical act.

Thus, in order to reinstate an equal status to delivery, we need to have students use body and voice combined for what I have named *full physical performance*. With such a combination, students (and teachers) can develop strategies in writing that have so far been overlooked.

Because many of the delivery activities are taken from theater perform-ance, I will also be utilizing terminology from that area, such as improvisa-tion and role-playing. In fact, these two terms themselves are so often used in this chapter section, they need to be defined and thoroughly discussed here first.

Improvisation

Improvisation is spontaneous composing and performing on the spur of the moment and without any preparation. Performers are provided with minimal details about the situation, character, and purpose of an exercise, then asked to react in the appropriate manner. Improvisations are excellent tools for brainstorming new ideas, making revisions, and for employing full physical performance in the writing classroom.

According to drama teacher Gerald Chapman, improvisation should follow a few simple rules:

1. Keep the instructions to a bare minimum. Just say who, what, and why. Avoid psychological detail. Do not ascribe any qualities to the characters: let the students write the situation by writing their own characters, and vice versa.

2. Keep it short.

3. Everything that happens is valid so long as the students accept it as real, make it real, and remain in role. Be careful not to insist on a conventional or predeter-mined reaction.

4. Regard improvisations as part of the process of writing rather than as an acting exercise. Don't let the quality of the acting get in the way of analyzing the choices made by the writers. Introduce the idea of revision and rewriting by referring to each improvisation as a further draft. Transform the spontaneity of the improv into a draft that can be reread and rewritten. (44)

Nellie McCaslin uses the term *creative drama* for improvisation. She states that this technique may make use of an entire story with a beginning, middle, and end, or it may explore, develop, and express ideas and feelings in short dramatic enactments, but it is always improvised. Dialogue is created by the students; lines are never written down or memorized. With each enactment, the story becomes more detailed and better organized, but it always remains extemporaneous and is at no time designed for an audience. The actors are guided by a leader, not necessarily a director, whose purpose is the optimal growth and development of the players (5).

In my use of the term improvisation, the reenactment of each student's ideas or essays are for an audience and do eventually become written. After all, this creative activity is designed to lead to a polished essay. Moreover, improvisation implements delivery in the classroom by having the students use their voices and bodies to give movement and sound to their ideas. To that end, following are several activities based on my understanding of improvisation.

Activity (variation on Chapman 45): Ask for two participants. The first person to speak says whatever he or she likes on any issue and the second person disagrees with whatever the statement was. For instance, the first person may make a comment on a local election to which the second person will disagree. Allow the exchange to last several minutes or until the participants run out of steam. Discuss with the class what happened. What was the disagreement? Was there a real disagreement? Who presented the most logical arguments? What was missing from either argument? What other arguments could be added to these two? A variation of this exercise would be to have several more participants join the disagreement one at a time, bringing new sides to the issue or joining in on one side against another.

Activity (Chapman 79): Have students bring in newspaper clippings on any current affair, such as court cases, environmental issues, and so on. Quote a line or two from the article as the first line of an improvisation. Have the students react to the line either as the speaker or as various members involved in the event. After a set amount of time, lead class discussion about what occurred. A role-playing variation on this exercise would be to assign certain students as various characters involved in the current affair they are discussing. Set the scene and have the participants react to each other.

Dramatizations of current affairs could become springboards for argumentative or persuasive essays and may be implemented during any step of the writing process. The purpose of these two exercises is to show that all issues have more than one side by obtaining feedback to students' own ideas during the writing process. The practices not only prepare students to write more convincing arguments, but also enable them to see how concrete details, facts, and examples are essential in getting someone else to see their own side of the issue. These activities could come at any stage of the writing process. As an invention tool, they give students ideas for prewriting; during drafting, they can clarify some points and give students the other side of an issue; for revision, they can show students details or counterarguments they may have overlooked. In fact, after final drafts are complete, teachers may even have a follow-up discussion in which students take sides according to their own essays. Teachers can ask questions such as "How did your views change, if at all?" "What types of counterarguments were used?" "Where will the issue go in the future?" Because the activities make use of performance, both voice and body, delivery is reintegrated in the writing class.

Activity (Swartz 93): Have students collect newspaper or magazine headlines that have been published in the past week or month. Students work in pairs, each pair being given (or drawing from a bag) one headline. They must then decide upon the story that might have accompanied that headline. To go along with the story, students create a tableau that would represent the photograph that would accompany the headline. These stories may be developed into news bulletins for television.

Similar to the previous activities, this one not only dramatizes current affairs, but also any historical event that has current interest. Students learn to attempt a more objective approach to reporting a story and get a chance to see meanings behind each story. The tableaux, too, help tell the story, getting other students to think about one important aspect of the event. Here, we see delivery incorporated in the writing process with the use of the body through the tableaux and voice through the discussion/news report.

Activity (Swartz 61): Have the students imagine they work for an advertising agency and they have been asked to write and perform a one-minute TV or radio commercial for a controversial issue. The students can perform the commercial live in the class or, for those with access to equipment, they can actually record their commercial for viewing (or listening) in the class.

Here, students are forced to be aware of their audience's likes and dislikes and where that audience may stand on the issue in question. Besides, the students learn that they need to appeal to those audience interests in order to persuade them quickly. With the shortness of the ad, the students need to be succinct; they learn they cannot fit much into a 1-minute spot. In addition, the exercise makes the students research the issue so that they are aware of the most important aspects, those which need to be covered in the short ad. This activity may be used as a writing assignment in itself or as part of the prewriting and research leading to a longer essay. Delivery is represented in this activity through the performance of the ad.

Word Play.   How often have students handed in essays that read as if they had made a copy of a thesaurus? Many times, students use words without paying any attention to their true meaning. They believe that being in college means writing with "big" words, and unfortunately, their essays end up being confusing and unclear. In the following activities, teachers can utilize delivery in making the students more aware of their vocabulary. That is, by incorporating performance, more physicality than simply mind and hand, the students can learn both the efficacy of "small" words and precise meanings of more difficult vocabulary.

> **Activity** (Knabe 45): Discuss with students words that reflect various personalities, such as belligerent, arrogant, devious, and so forth. Then have them create characters based on people drawn from their own experience who typify such words.

This activity not only helps students with the meaning of words, but also works with their descriptions of people. Good as a prewriting exercise for a narrative essay, this activity requires students to use their own memories to role-play people they have known. Because they are role-playing, using their voices and bodies, delivery is present in the process.

> **Activity** (Knabe 45): Ask students to make a list of words that are most often associated with special days such as July 4th, Christmas, Easter, and so on. Then they improvise situations that are not related to those special occasions but depict the words the students used to characterize such holidays.

In order to help students expand on their word definitions, this exercise attempts to get students to put words in other contexts. Moreover, using such improvisation helps in breaking the stereotypes that the words may conjure up for students. At the same time, this activity promotes delivery through the use of performance.

> **Activity** (Knabe 45): Determine which words in a given subject are used most frequently, for instance in political science—government, democracy, constitution; in biology—microscope, specimen, culture; in literature—stanza, theme, paraphrase. Give the students a list of the roots from which such words are built. Have the students dramatize the roots.

Expanding a student's vocabulary aids in getting rid of clichés and worn-out phrases in their writing. Having them dramatize the root word affords them a way of visualizing the origin of such words and as a way of preparing the student to meet the root in related words. With this activity, students learn roots and origins of words, which help in their writing and in their reading. Delivery is also present here because the students must dramatize the words.

> **Activity** (Knabe 45): In *The Belle of Amherst*, Emily Dickinson is portrayed as saying, "Now, there's a word you take your hat off to!" Ask students to find a word they would "take their hat off to," then place their word in a hat. Have each student draw a word from the hat, discover its meaning, write the word on the board, and mime its meaning for the class.

Again, this exercise not only helps students expand their vocabulary, but also aids in getting them to use the word correctly, and what better way to remember a new word than from a peer's mime, which also fulfills the need for delivery in this instance.

Interviewing. The *interview*, a type of improvisation, is a versatile tool for group or individual use and can be accomplished in many forms and configurations. The basic points to observe are that there is an assigned interviewer(s) and an interviewee(s). Topics can range from media representatives questioning government officials on some controversial topic, to students questioning professionals about careers, or to students practicing at job interviewing. Interviews provide a means to aid reflection about a topic, involving the consideration of relevant questions and the pressure to supply relevant answers. They also encourage a serious response, pointing out contrasting viewpoints and perspectives.

> **Activity** (Pfister and Petrick 217): Pair the students and ask them to write a character sketch that would capture the "essence" of their partners. Allow an hour of class time for the teams to question each other, giving them the option to continue the interview outside of class time. Have the students present their sketches to the class as a way of introduction. Also ask each student to write an evaluation of the sketch about him/her. The evaluation may address any points the student considered pertinent, such as factual accuracy, sincerity of tone, etc.

Although this activity does not employ role-playing or improvisation, it is a great icebreaker for the first or second day of class. It introduces the students to one another, gets them started writing immediately, and gives them experience in isolating information. The evaluations of the profiles and introductions also provide partners with an immediate, tangible reaction to their writing from a real audience, and, with the performance of ideas, the students reintegrate delivery in the classroom.

Activity: The topic is a controversial waste incinerator proposed for the student's hometown. In pairs, students have a choice of how they want to set up their interview: one student is to be a media representative (TV, radio, newspaper, magazine) and the other chooses to be a government official, an entrepreneur funding the facility, or a townsperson for or against the incinerator. The students have 5 to 10 minutes to prepare questions and possible answers according to their role in the interview. Then the actual interview can last about fifteen to twenty minutes (as needed), after which students write a brief summary of what occurred during the interview. These summaries are shared with the class and the various viewpoints are discussed. From here, the students are to write an expository essay about the incinerator, using several of the viewpoints given.

When students are paired in this activity, they get a more personal chance at sharing views instead of as part of an entire class discussion, but this does not lessen the fact that the inclusion of voice and body fulfills the need for delivery. Even on a minor scale as between a team of two, if the students utilize voice, body, or voice and body, delivery is present.

The exercise is probably best suited to the beginning steps of the writing process but could probably be adapted to a revision activity in which the students share the views they have found that dominate their essays.

Activity: In pairs, students may practice for possible job interviews. One student is assigned a role as the executive of a company, and the other student is the prospective employee. Again, students have 5 to 10 minutes to prepare questions (from employer and employee viewpoints). The actual interview may last from twenty to thirty minutes (as needed), after which each student (still in role) writes a summary of the interview stating whether or not he or she will offer or take the position, and why. The interviewers likewise write whether or not they would hire this person and why. The students then share their summaries during a class discussion. To conclude the assignment, students write, as themselves again, their impressions of the interview process and what they can expect from a real experience.

Besides offering students a chance to better their writing ability through observation and interaction, like the previous activity, this practical exercise offers them a chance to develop interviewing skills that they will need later. It also gives them a chance to critique their own actions and reactions in such a situation. Similarly, this activity could be utilized when students are writing resumes and job application letters, something that is common in many writing classes. Delivery is represented here through the physicality of the interview and class discussion.

Activity (Personal communication with Paul Fischer on February 27, 1992): This is an activity that the teacher takes part in. Begin class as usual. Several minutes into the class, another person (compatriot) comes to the class searching for a missing book (paper, name sheet, etc.). This person causes quite a disturbance and eventually he or she and the teacher become embroiled in an improvised argument. All of this transpires for the students' benefit as if it were real. After a while, the person slams out of the room, and the teacher tells the students to report in writing what they have just seen while he or she chases after the compatriot. Give the students several minutes to first discuss the happening among themselves (which they surely will do) and to write the report. Upon returning to the class, the teacher has the students interview him or her in order to add to their report.

Such an activity really enlivens a classroom. First, the students are totally taken by surprise and once over the initial shock, they cannot help but to talk to one another, as neighbors at the scene of an accident. Most important, this activity gives the students experience in observation and reporting. Their reports and subsequent interview of the teacher could lead to practice in news reporting, both written and live. (Some students may opt to give their report as if on television.) Of course, this activity is well suited for prewriting and represents delivery through the teacher's role-playing, the students' discussion, and the subsequent interview.

Activity (Personal communication with Sue Carter Simmons on February 15, 1992): Before teaching a session on tone, announce to the class that their formal reports, presentations, or research papers are due two weeks earlier than previously announced. Then have an "emergency" for which you need to leave the room. Ask the students to write a quick memo or letter stating what they thought about the new earlier due date. Later, have students read the letters aloud in class.

Similar to the previous activity, this exercise should shock and most likely anger the students. They will discuss the problem among themselves first and then probably write a scathing letter about moving up due dates. Although this activity was originally used in a technical writing class prior to a session on business letters, it still is useful in teaching tone in any writing class. The exercise also fulfills the need for delivery in the classroom by incorporating discussion and reading aloud as well as the teacher's small improvisation.

Activity (Swartz 39): This can be done after having an improvisation or any other performance that the students watched but didn't necessarily take part in (like the Fischer activity). Have the students work in pairs. One person is working for the media and must "get the story" for his or her respective medium. (You can even assign them specific jobs, such as anchor for NBC, reporter for *The Washington Post*, etc.) The other student is a witness to the drama. Have students set up the interview and role-play for 5 to 10 minutes. Then have people switch pairs and roles; the interviewers become interviewees with a new partner. Have them write the results of the interviews into news stories.

As with the previous activities, this exercise also hones observation and description skills as well as interviewing abilities. By switching roles, the students get a chance to see events from different perspectives. This exercise is also suited to prewriting. Delivery is present in this activity through the original improvisation and the interviews.

Activity (Swartz 87): A local radio (or TV) show has been following the developments of a local issue. The students can work in groups of five or six to conduct a talk show interview, covering the various points of view of the citizens within the community. The students can decide which roles they want to take and which questions they feel the interviewer should ask.

Once again, this activity aids students in seeing other viewpoints as well as answering questions about the issue being discussed. Like the other interviewing exercises, this one is good for prewriting. However, it may also be utilized as a tool during the writing and revision stages. The students have investigated the topic to a degree and begun their prewriting before taking part in the exercise. During the activity, the students take notes on other viewpoints, and immediately following the discussion, they write their essays (or revise). Because the students use performance in role-playing and interviews, delivery is fulfilled by this activity.

Activity (Personal communication with Alice Calderonello on February 20, 1992): Based on any of the popular television talk shows (Oprah, Donahue, etc.), and similar to the previous activity, this exercise begins with the entire class suggesting different topical issues, then voting on which issue to use for the assignment. The class is then divided into five groups (depending on size of class), each group having one student who will volunteer to play a member on the talk show panel. Each group decides on the character that their panel member will be in terms of occupation, race, and sex. (There should be characters of varying backgrounds, for instance, a physical education teacher, a minister, a school board member, etc.) Then each group must construct the character their volunteer is to play, deciding on his or her position about the issue. Each group must also write a synopsis of the character to be used as an introduction for the show. The characters may even dress the part. When the show takes place, the entire class is involved after the first introductions. People ask questions, discuss the issue, and, in general, have fun. As the final assignment, students must write an editorial for their local newspaper, either as a panelist or as an audience member, stating their position on the issue.

This assignment has several benefits: it discusses issues that are currently relevant to students' lives; allows the class full participation from beginning of the activity to the final essay; permits freedom in creativity with the forming of the panel characters; shows the students the various sides of an issue, something they need in order to write a fully developed essay; and gives them experience in audience awareness. In addition, through the activity's extravagant role-playing and the subsequent question–answer format, delivery is reflected through the performance.

Meetings

Also a form of improvisation, meetings can get the whole class involved, including the teacher (optional). The class can be turned into a town, a parish, tribe, local government, faculty, protesters, social workers, and so on. Once again, meetings can demonstrate the range of viewpoints on any issue. Plus, meetings are a useful way to introduce a "disturbance" into an established order, encouraging suggestions for dealing with such a disturbance (Neelands 63). The following are examples of assignments that utilize the meetings format.

Activity: Using the incinerator topic again, divide the class into five groups (depending on size): local government, health care officials, people proposing the incinerator, townspeople for the project, and townspeople against the project. The agenda for the meeting is that each group has 5 minutes to present its point of view to the local government board. Then the meeting is opened to discussion. (The students should have about 5 minutes to prepare their statements.) After the discussion (usually very heated), the students should freewrite for 5 to 10 minutes on what happened. These freewrites are shared and the class discusses the various viewpoints from the meeting. The assignment is to write an expository essay using the various viewpoints.

Activity: The topic is the freedom to choose courses for an individualized major versus a required core curriculum. The meeting should consist of four groups: students, faculty, administration, and local business people. Again, each group should have some time to discuss its stand. (Groups do not have to arrive at a consensus.) The meeting can be opened with a general statement about its purpose (to decide whether the college needs more freedom, or a core curriculum) and then discussion can ensue from there. After the discussion, students should jot down their impressions of the meeting and then share them with the class. From here, the assignment is to write an expository essay on core curriculum versus freedom of choice using the various viewpoints from the meeting.

Comparable to the interview activities, these exercises give students the benefit of different views on the issue as well as a chance to voice their own opinion in the guise of another character. Instead of having one-to-one pairings or just a few people role-playing, the entire class gets a chance to improvise during the meeting. These practices may, furthermore, be adapted to all steps of the writing process. For the intermediate writing step, after the groups are assigned and before the town meeting, have them collaboratively write a summary of their position on the issue, including any descenting opinions. After the meeting, the group should revise the summary, including any counterarguments they thought were important to the issue. Of course, delivery is represented here by the use of improvisation.

Gerry Brookes uses town meeting sessions as a strategy for including speaking in his writing classroom. His format is to have one or two students scheduled each week for a 3-minute talk on a topic they care about. The teacher models the activity first by speaking perhaps on the thoughtless ways students ask to get into closed courses. When each speaker is finished, the class applauds and Brookes asks questions: "In thinking or writing about this subject, what else might the speaker take into account" (3)? This allows students to offer support, point out misjudgments of audience, suggest alternative points of view while quelling any open disagreement. If confrontation does threaten, Brookes turns it aside by restating the students' comments or asking for other points of view. Other questions include: "If this person were to do something about this subject in writing, what might he or she do? Who is the audience for this talk? What other kinds of writing might come out of this session" (4)? The idea here is to give students a chance to speak on an issue of their own choosing without fear of face-to-face confrontation, or without the class becoming involved in a long, extended discussion, but Brookes adds that the attention to the speaker and his or her topic helps to prevent "the disappointment and deflation caused by moving directly to the next speaker" (4). He believes that his town meetings serve as an invention and revision strategy by suggesting arguments and evidence that have not yet been taken into account and by offering ideas for new or related topics, both for speakers and audience. I view these sessions as another application of delivery in the writing classroom. Students speak out, off the cuff, or with a manuscript, physically presenting their topic to their peers for the advantage of both the speaker/writer and his or her audience. In addition, the second question, "Who is the audience for this talk?" leads to how or whether the writer actually will deliver the writing to another real audience.

Role-Playing

When students (or teachers) see the world through someone else's eyes, they show the outer aspects of that person and understand how that person thinks and feels. This is the strategy of *role-playing*, which provides a structure for the student's exploration of human behavior (Morgan and Saxton 38). Role-playing is very similar to improvisation. (In fact, several drama instructors made no differentiation between the two.) Like improvisation, role-playing brings delivery to the classroom because students and teacher incorporate their whole selves—mind, voice, and body—by dramatizing writing.

For our purposes here, role-playing is a more structured, character-oriented improvisation. That is, when role-playing, the character is more fully outlined for the student than if she were simply told to play, say, an "old woman giving her opinions" in an improvisation. Instead, in a role-playing situation, the student may be told that her character is 78 years old, a widowed mother of three living in a nursing home in Atlanta, and has always voted Republican. As well, in my concept of role-playing, students may be given time to rehearse parts, perhaps several days, whereas improvisation usually takes place immediately. Also, role-playing may or may not have a developed script.

In addition, the teacher can often take on a role, especially when attempting to further the students' discussions. If a group of players is floundering or simply not working, a teacher may ask the pertinent questions or add the needed information the students lack to get them back on track. For instance, the assignment is for a group to be a jury deliberating over a murder verdict. If one group is obviously working superficially, instead of the teacher merely reminding them of the assignment, she could adopt a juror's role and state: "The murder weapon was never found. How can we be sure this person is to blame?" By taking on a role, the teacher is not only guiding the students into their roles and reinforcing the task at hand, but also enriching the material (Morgan and Saxton 39).

Activity (Rubin and Dodd 13): Have students role-play conflict situations in groups of four. The students each have a turn playing one of four roles in each situation. After each student has a turn at all four roles, a group discussion focuses on the different perspectives of the same situation. Then assign essays in

which students write from a point of view that reconciles the various perspectives.

This activity is designed to help students decenter and to see that situations
have many perspectives. The role-switching is an excellent preparation for
persuasive or argumentative essays. However, the scenarios developed in
this exercise may also lead to narratives, descriptions, and exposition. That
is, students gain insight into various viewpoints and have immediate audience feedback for their own ideas and essential details. At the same time,
delivery is incorporated into the process because students use performance
in exemplifying their ideas.

In setting up for this activity, the teacher will want to devise each
situation, then hand out role cards (index cards on which are written the
role of one character in the group). The students improvise their dialogue
until they have worked through the problem or until the instructor thinks
they have done an adequate job, after which they pass their cards to the left
and, without a pause, begin another round of role-playing. (For examples of
scenarios and roles, see Appendix C).

> **Activity** (Swartz 49): In pairs, students can choose one or more of these
> situations to role-play in order to better understand problem solving. Partners
> decide on who plays which role. Arguments should be conducted without
> disturbing other students.
>
> - You and your friend want to go to a movie. One of you wants to see a slapstick
>   comedy and the other wants to see an action-thriller. What will you do?
> - Your friend wants to work on a project with you, but the last time you worked
>   together you did most of the work. What do you do?
> - Your friend has lost his or her wallet and thinks you might have taken it. What
>   will you say?
> - Your friend wants to borrow a cassette tape by your favorite group, but the
>   last time he or she did so, it was returned in bad condition. Will you lend it
>   this time?
> - You haven't spoken to your friend for over a week. Each of you is waiting for
>   the other to apologize. What will you do?
> - You spent your last $50 that was supposed to be for food on a new coat. Your
>   parents said the money would have to last you for the rest of the semester.
>   What will you do?
> - You borrowed your friend's car to do some errands, and while driving, you ran
>   into the back end of a van. What do you do?

The students can repeat any of the situations by switching roles in order to
experience the other person's point of view. After the discussions, the students

write summaries of what took place and how the pair went about solving the problem.

Again, like the previous role-play activity, this exercise is good in showing point of view and getting immediate audience feedback. Moreover, it gives students insights into problem-solving activities, something they will need to use not only in other courses, but also in later life. This exercise is a great prelude to teaching a "Proposing a Solution" essay (an essay in which the students propose a solution to a problem with which they are fairly familiar). That is, it makes the students think through a problem and several possible solutions at the same time, gaining feedback from an audience that may have opposing viewpoints. Likewise, in using that performance to elicit feedback, the students also utilize delivery in their writing process.

> **Activity** (Friday and Beranek 5): For a final oral presentation, groups of three to five students must employ some dramatic scene, role play and poetry reading in a 45 minute problem-solving presentation complete with visuals, handouts, and persuasive tactics to sell the solution. The group should also hand in a collaboratively written summary of their presentation.

This adaptation of the previous activity provides poetic elements that can bring eloquence, grace, excitement, and power to the logical proof besides offering students the experience of problem solving. The students must research the topic thoroughly and know their audience in order to provide the correct appeal to sell their solution. For instance, if the topic was the ozone layer, the students may present several solutions through a dramatic scene depicting a burned out civilization, and their poetry may come from Thoreau or Emerson, or even more contemporary poets. As with the other activities of this section, delivery is fulfilled here by the use of performance, the addition of voice and body to the writing process.

Role-playing and improvisation are used consistently throughout the remainder of the chapter. They take on various interpretations and adaptations, but when the terms are used, they generally can still be defined as previously described. For more discussions of role-playing and improvisation, see Heathcote's *Collected Writings on Education and Drama* (1984) and Spolin's *Improvisation for the Theatre* (1963).

Documentary

The documentary can be used to present information about some topic to the rest of the class. This may incorporate a variety of modes, such as interviews, tableaux, improvisation, and so on. Documentaries allow for expert roles in the class; because it requires some research, each student can become an expert on some topic or an aspect of one topic. The documentary also provides the possibility of collage, several students presenting their information through several improvisations linked together in some format. Thus, students are able to approach meaning in a variety of ways, including small groups who contribute their own interests and enthusiasm (Neelands 62). An example of a documentary assignment follows:

> **Activity:** Have the students suggest topics or issues they are interested in and compile a list so that each student may choose one of those topics without having two people doing the same thing. Then the students must try to find as much information as possible about that topic to fill at least a twenty-minute presentation in class. Divide the students into groups in which they will discuss how best to present their information to the class. The presentation should not simply be a speech. With the help of the group members, each student will incorporate improvisation, tableaux, interview, and so on, in order to present the information. Following the presentation, the students must write a summary of their information using feedback from their group members.

This documentary provides the students with an audience while preparing their presentation and during the writing of the summary. More important, however, it allows students to be experts in one area so that when the topic arises again in discussion during the semester, the class may look to him or her for information. A variation of this exercise is to have the students as a group choose one topic and have each member of the group choose a portion of the topic on which to become an expert. The presentation is then done as a group effort, as is the follow-up summary. Here, delivery is reintegrated into the classroom because the students use speech and performance to fulfill the assignment.

> **Activity** (Friday and Beranek 13): Students choose a famous speech and do research on the speaker. Each student dramatically presents the speech, prefaced with a historical overview and observations on the rhetorical aspects of the situation. The research essay is handed in also.

Like the previous activity, this exercise has students become experts on one person and one specific speech. It provides experience in researching, and in discerning the relative facts surrounding the speech. If the student is resourceful, this activity allows some fun with historical costumes. The dramatic presentation also provides the students with delivery to a real audience.

Talk–Write

As I mentioned in chapter 2, Zoellner is also a proponent of reinstating a more physical approach to writing in his classroom. Since his original monograph in 1969 about his theory of talk–write, many other teachers have adapted his model to their classrooms. Therefore, I have dedicated one section entirely to his ideas and their later incarnations.

For many of the following activities, the classroom should look more like an art studio. Zoellner's ideal room would look like such: Nearly all the desks and chairs are eliminated. Large blackboards wrap around the entire perimeter of the room. In the open floor space are large freestanding, movable blackboards, or large pads of blank newsprint mounted on freestanding easels, with felt pens or similar marking devices that have broad strokes so all writing could have length-of-the-room visibility.

This unique classroom is designed for many types of dialogue, including that between teacher and entire class. More importantly, the dialogue could be between pairs of students, teacher and small group, teacher and single student, student and entire class, or groups of three or four students, each of these groups working at its own chalkboard or easel. The writing is marked large enough to be seen at a distance, and the teacher simply moves about the room, commenting, evaluating, and suggesting in much the same way as an art instructor. As the students speak their essays, they write them out, experimenting with the words that most closely approximate what they are saying aloud to their audience. This arrangement not only gives them immediate feedback from whomever they are working with, but also reinforces a strong sense of the plasticity and fluidity of our language. Another great advantage to this setup is that the students can have the "kinesthetic satisfaction of obliterating his chalkboard mistakes with the swipe of an eraser, or listening to the resounding rip of newsprint as he tears the top sheet off the pad to give himself a fresh start" (Zoellner 299).

However, Zoellner's art studio look is an ideal, and given strained budgets and other administrative headaches, teachers may have to settle for the chalkboards they have and perhaps butcher paper on easels placed strategically in the room. Nevertheless, the idea can be the same: students and teacher working physically, beyond the mere hand and mind of the traditional classroom, involving more delivery in the process of writing.

Activity (Wixon and Wixon 129): Pair students at a section of chalkboard or at butcher paper/newsprint, with a wide felt-tip pen. Each team includes a questioner and a writer. Have the writers talk out what they want to write, with encouragement from the questioners by asking natural questions such as "What happened next?" and "I'm confused. Try again." When the team has enough information, the writer starts writing while talking out each section before writing. During the writing (could be a sentence at a time), the questioners serve as reminders of details and order, clarifiers, adders; simply the questioners are the people who keep the writers talking. When complete, the writers read the essay aloud so the questioners may comment. Then the questioners read it aloud so the writers may hear it in another voice. Finally the partners switch roles and begin on the second essay, repeating the preceding steps.

Of course, with this activity, the paper or chalkboards will look messy with crossouts, reordered sentences and paragraphs, and changes in spelling and mechanics, but the important thing is that the students make the crossover from speaking aloud to writing through delivery. That is, they are using not only their minds and hands, but also their whole bodies in talking out the writing as the process progresses.

Activity (Meyers 15): Have paired students sit facing each other, with pen and paper close by so notes may be taken. One student acts as speaker and the other as listener. The speakers talk out their ideas, exploring and explaining. The listeners provide positive reinforcement by listening attentively, asking questions and giving feedback. Allow students to speak for thirty minutes about the assignment, discussing scope, audience, purpose, style, tone, etc., each student talking through his or her solution to a rhetorical problem. Next, students take ten minutes to make notes on what they can use in their essay from the conversation.

For this activity, the teacher does not need the elaborate set up of Zoellner's classroom, but the idea behind it is the same; students talk out their ideas and then write what they have spoken about. Here, we have the voice alone added to the mind and hand (as in the first section of this chapter), and again, we have delivery implemented through that voicing.

Activity (Gilbertsen and Killingsworth 110–12): Familiarize the students with the chosen stylistic goal of the exercise, for instance, eliminating short choppy sentences. Pair the students, hand out a set of about six sentences that require revising or combining. One student is the primary editor or rewriter, and the other is secondary editor and auditor. With each new set of assigned material, the pair reverse roles. The team discusses thoroughly the material to be revised, talking through problems and giving alternative revisions. If disagreement arises, the primary editor has the final say. When finished, the team proofreads its work. Only the secondary editor brings the material to you. If the work is satisfactory, approach both team members and make positive comments before they switch roles for the next exercise. If the work falls short, ask the secondary editor the rationale behind the rewriter's choices. If the student's explanation does not change your mind, circle the areas that could be strengthened. Be careful not to force your stylistic choices on the team, but make sure the secondary editor understands the goals of the exercise. Then he or she must explain your remarks to the primary editor before they rework the exercise.

Teachers should remember to always model the process first; that is, before matching the teams but after explaining the mechanics of the process, the teacher should model the behavior by running through the procedure on the board. In addition, while teams are working, the teacher may make suggestions to pairs that seem blocked, asking questions about team choices. Intervention provides further modeling, showing students how to talk out difficult points and translate conversation into writing.

Although Gilbertsen and Killingsworth originally developed this activity for teaching technical editing, it can be useful for doing sentence combining or any grammar editing. This exercise is also useful to our context here in that it incorporates speaking with writing, thus using delivery to spur the learning of style.

Activity (Zoellner 297): During conferences, have a large chalkboard next to your desk for students when they are having difficulty putting together the words for their assignment.

Although this is not exactly an activity for the classroom, Zoellner's idea for the teacher's office and the way in which it functions is an implementation of delivery. For instance, when the teacher asks a student what she meant by a certain sentence or paragraph and the student ably talks out the meaning, the teacher can point to the board and say "Good! Write that down!" Once the revision is on the board, the teacher and the student can turn their attention to any ambiguities in meaning that may crop up because of translating vocal emission into scribal modality. The teacher can lead the student to come up with a vocal statement that eliminates or reduces the ambiguity and have her instantly write this on the board. Through judicious questioning, the teacher can lead the student to the vocal assertion of an implication, assumption, or logical consequence of what has already been written, all of it adding to what is on the chalkboard. Eventually, students end up with a paragraph, or sentence cluster, which says, in their own words (not yours), what they really had in mind when they wrote that first opaque paragraph. With such movements and voicing, this practice reinstates delivery to the writing process.

According to Gary Hatch, this method can also be adjusted to work over the phone. Students simply read their essay, the teacher asks pertinent questions, students answer the questions and immediately write down what they say. Finally, they read back what they have written and the teacher gives the appropriate comments (cited in Hatch and Walters 346).

Miscellaneous Delivery

The activities in the preceding subdivisions of this section have all fit neatly into various categories. However, I have also compiled some exercises for delivery that do not easily suit any specific category. All the same, they are still viable activities to reincorporate delivery in the classroom. I present them here, in no certain order, for the benefit of teachers and their students.

Activity (Chapman 6): Have a student strike a match and describe his or her life history while the match remains alight between the fingers.

This exercise has two objectives: it introduces students to the concept of storytelling and to the need for careful selection of material. The burning match enforces economy of expression while giving the students an action on which everything depends. After everyone has had a chance to tell their stories, then the assignment is to write that same story on paper, with the same economy of words. One adaptation is to tape record all the students on their own tape for their use while writing the summary.

Another variation of this exercise is to ask students to make paper airplanes, then while the planes are in flight to describe their lives or their greatest ambitions. The match is premade and easily controlled, but a paper airplane has to be expertly crafted before it can fly. Any technical errors can dash the most poetic life histories. Both of these activities fulfill the delivery theory in that they use voice and body for the assignment.

Activity (Swartz 23): Have students stand in two rows facing each other (or students can work in pairs). Each student is to observe the person opposite and make note of dress, hair, eyes, and so on. Then instruct the students to turn their backs on each other, whereupon each student changes one thing about his or her appearance (i.e. combs hair differently, removes glasses, unbuttons jacket). Students again face each other and make note of what their partners have changed. If the students cannot guess the change after one minute, their partners reveal the answers. Repeat the activity with students making two changes, then three or four changes.

Like several previous exercises, the purpose of this activity is to hone observation skills. It can be used as a warm up to narrative writing in which students so often lack enough detail. Delivery is present here with the use of the whole body in the practice.

> **Activity** (Friday and Beranek 3): As warm up sessions for workshops, have students read aloud selections from poetry using some emphasis, suspense, and sense of personality.

Similar to the reading aloud in the dramatizing voice alone section, this activity differs in that the material used is not the students' own writing, and they are reading with more of a dramatic flair, more of a physical performance than simply reading aloud. Such practice should sharpen diction, improve voice, facilitate facial expression and gesture, and improve poise and confidence. Most of all, such study helps students to develop the ability to think on their feet under stress. This activity we could say is a warm up to improvisation and role-playing. It gets the students used to talking in front of others without having to make up the dialogue. With the addition of performance and the oral presentation in this activity, delivery is reincorporated into the classroom.

> **Activity** (Donlan 2): Have students overhear and record from memory an argument and then use it as the basis for a short one-act radio, television or stage play.

How many times have we eavesdropped on conversations just for entertainment? For the students, this activity gives them a goal for that eavesdropping. The purpose behind the activity is to strengthen the students' ears for dialogue, something they need for narratives but of which they so often do not have a grasp. This exercise is also very well suited to a creative writing classroom. Delivery is represented here through the performance of the assignment.

> **Activity** (Hogg 13): Have the students recall a sense memory of a particular smell, taste, touch, sight, or sound that they remember from their childhood days and tell their memory stories to their peer group. Then choose several of the senses to act out as a group. After the group acting, have all the students write about what they have seen and heard, and their reaction to it.

> **Activity** (Hogg 13): Have the students listen to a sound effects recording and try to identify the sounds, then have them create a story using only the sounds they heard from the recording.

Activity (Hogg 13): Pass around bags with objects in them that are strange to the touch. They can only feel the objects, not look in the bags. Then have the students identify what the objects are by writing descriptive sentences about what they are feeling in the bags. Have them create a story using the objects and share them with the class. The same exercise can be performed for sense of smell, or taste.

So often, students tend to forget that there are five senses and, when writing details in essays, usually concentrate only on sight. These activities are ways in which to have students hone skills for the other senses. Good for narrative writing, these practices also allow students to think about their memories in terms of an audience. The students can learn what details are necessary when telling their stories and what exactly appeals to their audience. The activities can be prewriting exercises or even intermediate writing tasks: students would tell their stories as they write them for the audience. By their very nature, these activities that employ the senses represent delivery in the classroom. If the students use only one of the senses (besides the touch of the paper and pen), this is incorporating the body beyond mind and hand in the writing process.

Activity (Lutz 37): Hold class in a room equipped with carpet and comfortable chairs and couches. Have hard, uncomfortable folding chairs set up in lines in the room. When they first arrive, tell students to sit in the folding chairs, sitting straight, folded hands in their laps, quiet and listening. Play several diverse pieces of music, for instance, Ravel's "Bolero," some Gregorian chants, Jefferson Airplane, AC-DC, the Doors, Barry Manilow, Simon and Garfunkle. At the end of the period, students simply leave the room. The next class is held in the same room without the folding chairs. The students may sit or lie wherever they want. Close the drapes, turn off the lights, light a candle in the middle of the room and a few sticks of incense. With these conditions, play the same music as before. Again, when the period was over, the students simply leave. The following class, held back in the normal classroom, ask students to write about the two experiences; were there differences, why and what did they feel both times? Copy the responses, distribute and discuss.

William Lutz claims that after he used this exercise, student discussion centered on being sensitive to the world around them and being aware of using all senses, not just one or two. From this, the students extrapolated that the writer must use more than just the eye. Like the previous activities, students need to be reminded that there are five senses and, in writing, detailed descriptions of those senses are needed to invoke the readers' imaginations. Also as stated before, because this activity involves the senses, it automatically involves delivery.

> **Activity** (Lutz 38): Have students put their desks in a circle, turn off the lights and conduct a discussion in the dark, after which the students should write about the experience. When the students have adjusted to the situation, once again, they should write about it. Next, return to having the lights on for class discussion and have the students write about it. Selections from all three writing assignments should be copied and handed out.

When Lutz introduced this activity, the first reactions were obvious, that the feeling was "weird." Discussion centered on whether everyone had had the same experience, what each writer emphasized and were viewpoints the same (38). This exercise gets students to think about perspectives, making them view their world in a different way. It also gives them "food for thought," and, ultimately, ideas for writing. At the same time, it fulfills the need for delivery through the involvement of the body and voice.

> **Activity** (Lutz 36–37): Give out to each students an index card and instruct them not to read it until told to do so. Then at a given signal, the students read their cards and perform the activities described thereon (see Appendix D). At the end of three minutes, ask students to sit down and write as much as they can about what just occurred in the classroom, what they experienced and their reactions to it. Make copies of the students' descriptions and hand them out.

Lutz utilized the aforementioned activity on the second day of class. His students usually described the scene as unstructured chaos, but on further discussion, the students discovered that they had failed to perceive the organization that existed because of their own participation in an unfamiliar activity. Each student performs a different activity and, thus, has a totally different experience. The student staring at his or her feet had a different viewpoint than the one who was told to walk around the room and speak to everyone, and so on (36–37). Lutz states that later discussion of the activity included whether there was a principle of order in operation which the students had not seen; what is order and how truly orderly are our lives and the world (37)? If we take this idea one step further, what is meant by order in writing? In addition, through the use of the body in performing these various tasks, delivery is present in the classroom.

A CURRICULAR APPROACH TO DELIVERY

Thus far in this chapter, I have outlined many activities that teachers may use to reincorporate delivery in their classrooms, from voice only to full physicality. At this point, I want to conclude the chapter with some curricular approaches to delivery. As I stated before, the design James Moffett uses for his approach to teaching writing suggests ways of sequencing a series of related activities across time. I have followed Moffett's model with two lesson plans that illustrate how teachers can reinstate delivery for two specific writing assignments.

Moffett's Drama Model

James Moffett outlines a step-by-step process for what I have termed *dramatizing writing*, beginning with the use of voice alone through full physical performance. Although he has not used the term *delivery* nor attempted to tie in classical rhetorical history, his format for class includes physicality beyond the minds and hands of his students, and his own terminology takes its cue from the theater and performance. His use of words such as script, monologue, dialogue, and improvisation make his activities fit well with my theory of delivery. Therefore, I want to outline Moffett's strategies in temporal order so that teachers may see the progression from listening to a voice, to adding voice, to adding body, and, finally, to the full physicality of delivery. From this summary of Moffett's ideas, teachers may formulate their own ways of incorporating these and any of the other activities suggested in this chapter.

Moffett believes that people learn better if speaking, reading, listening and writing are closely interwoven (*Active Voice* 74). To substantiate his belief, he details a great many ways to incorporate performance in our composition classes. In his *Active Voice*, he details scripting, duologues, monologues, and dialogues as exercises in dramatizing writing.

In his use of performance in the composition class, Moffet begins with two modes of oral-to-written language: transcribing actual speech and scripting invented speeches. Transcribing gives the students valuable practice in rendering actual voices on paper and usually involves editing and summarizing. This practice helps the students bridge oral speech and written composition. On the other hand, scripting, where the writer simulates real speech by making up the roles, represents a sophisticated kind of composition (*Active Voice* 51). Therefore, scripting simply builds on the practice of transcribing. Students hear and practice writing down real speech, and then they practice making up their own for the writing roles that they need to play.

To apply his transcribing theory, Moffet (*Active Voice*) suggests five exercises for the classroom. After each exercise, I have included an explanation of how each aids a student's writing ability.

Oral Literature

Have each student write down any tale, joke, saying, jingle, verse, or song that he or she has heard by word of mouth. Then have them make a collection by asking other people for theirs—not just other students, but older people, and people from other backgrounds. The students should compile a booklet mixing types, or a booklet on each type such as yarns or sayings or jokes. They should leave blank pages for others to add theirs. Pass around the booklets and have students give copies to their contributors.

This activity gives students a chance to transcribe other people's speech. The students hear what is said and then write it down using the prerequisites of the written format. We could also say that this activity is a good way in which to possibly preserve oral traditions that we as a culture are losing. Furthermore, this activity represents delivery by the use of voice alone.

Survey

Have the students ask a number of people the same question or questions about something they want to know their view on, then have the students write a summary of what they learned. They could even depict results in a graph. Remind the students to think carefully about the questions they'll ask and whom they should approach. When writing the results, they must also keep in mind who they want to read these results. Include the summaries in a printout, newsletter, or local newspaper.

Surveying, like its predecessor, teaches the oral-to-written language lessons, but here, the students also learn various points of view, ways of composing questions, and techniques in compiling survey data, summarizing and audience awareness. At the same time, like the previous activity, the students incorporate delivery in the writing process through voice.

Interview

Students should choose an available person who is interesting for who he or she is, what he or she does, or special knowledge he or she has. Students should think of some questions to ask but be prepared to make up questions along the way as they hear answers to their first ones. They should tape and transcribe the interview and edit later, or take notes and write it up later. Either way, the students should summarize with occasional quotes, and think of who else might be interested in knowing what this person said and of how the students might best get the information to that person.

In addition to the benefits of the survey and of oral literature, from interviewing, students can learn how to gear questions to a specific person, that they should be prepared with some knowledge of the person they will interview, and how to do an interview properly. Other advantages include how to use quotes—where and when in writing—and how to take notes during an interview. Delivery is also present here through the interview itself.

Transcribing Discussions

Break the students into groups of three to five and have them discuss some topic from local events, from a class reading, a student's writing or the real life of one of the students. The topic could be a problem to solve, a controversy, an interesting idea or insight, or some issue that every one wants to explore. Have each group tape their discussion and transcribe it together later. Students can delete or add or alter lines. Groups should post the transcription or ask others to read it aloud to an audience who then discusses the ideas included. Or the students together may write a summary of their discussion that keeps all the main points and reads smoothly. Again, this may be posted, or delivered as a talk. This exercise can also be done for a panel discussion where each member represents a position or group to other people.

Besides giving students the practice of transcribing oral to written language, this activity also allows students to hear themselves alongside their peers and to practice revision after the fact. That is, after students hear or read the entire discussion, they may add or delete from their own ideas that they originally stated. This allows for students to expand on their ideas or to change their views once they have been influenced by others' thoughts. Here, too, we see the addition of more physicality than the first three exercises because we also have the suggestion that the discussion may be delivered as a talk or panel discussion with group members playing roles.

Transcribing Improvisation

Again, divide the class into groups of three to five. Each group decides on a main situation or story idea to improvise from and decides who plays which roles. (If students cannot come up with a topic, the teacher may have a list of topics to suggest.) The groups must also agree on the time and place for the action, establish the real or imagined presence of necessary props, then start a scene. Each group goes off by themselves where other classmates are not watching. There they make up dialogue and details of action as they go along by paying close attention both to what other players do and to what reactions are prompted within each of them. Students should ask themselves: "What are you and each of the others trying to do in the scene? What are your relationships to each other?"

Students can stop the action at any time, talk about what happened and how they might want to do it differently, then start again, making some of these changes until the composition of the scene is what seems best to them. They should play with factors. What difference would it make if the time or place or some other condition were changed, including who is present at the same time? Students can also recast who is playing which role, or even reverse roles. Another technique to employ is to have another person side-coach by feeding in observations and suggestions and stimuli that the actors heed without breaking the action.

Students should have a tape recorder running while playing and make a "take" of the version of the skit they like best. They should then transcribe the tape together to make a script to have other people act out or to perform themselves. All the scripts could be printed in one booklet for each class member.

This activity combines all the benefits of the other four, but, in addition, seems to be a culmination of them. It includes the most physicality of the five; the students role-play, transcribe the improvisation from a recording, and have another group act out the parts. This way, the students not only hear or read their own ideas and words, but they also get to see them in action. In this way, the activity incorporates delivery through full physical performance in aiding the students to get their points across to the audience.

Each of Moffet's transcribing exercises has elements of both voice and body delivering thoughts and ideas. These activities grow from oral speech into a written communication through a group effort. Along the way, students not only learn how a language changes from the oral form to the written form, but they also learn ways in which to get ideas, to see other people's views, and to understand the importance of details and accuracy. Furthermore, in the first three activities, the students expand their world beyond themselves, even beyond their classroom, to include people not usually associated with the class. Therefore, I believe all of these exercises would be well suited to prewriting or invention.

Moffet simultaneously uses each of the aforementioned exercises as a basis for his scripting practices, which follow.

Duologue

Instruct the students to invent or reproduce a conversation between two people by writing down just what each speaker says in turn. Have them write the conversation in script format, indicating action and setting by stage directions.

The time, place, and circumstances should be clear from what the conversants say. Length 800 to 1000 words, or a playing time of four to five minutes. The conversation should then be given to others to act out and may also be included in a booklet of plays.

Before executing this assignment, students should have the chance to improvise duologues with a partner, following the basic procedures in transcribing improvisation. Then, Moffet concludes, improvisation alone on paper will seem easier and more understandable to the student. Thus, the dynamics of interplay that the student learns through oral improvisation will make scripts more successful sooner by obviating too much negative reaction from the audience or the performers reading the script. However, according to Moffet, the scripts are interesting anyway, if not terribly dramatic, because performing writing itself enlivens composition for all concerned (53). As well, the performance of the conversation fulfills the need for delivery in the process.

One variant of this exercise is to eliminate stage directions and the script format, having the students write only what the characters say, making each speech a new paragraph. Character names may also be eliminated. Such exclusions leave more for the reader to infer and prepares the writer for invented monologues. Another variant is to increase the number of characters to three or four. Again, practice improvisation should precede the writing (54).

Subject matter for the duologue is unlimited and could turn in any direction. Moffet states that a narrative could form if the speakers are recalling events together; an essay could form if the conversation focuses on fairly impersonal ideas and generalities; or drama could form if the exchange becomes an interplay of personalities. The class can discover for themselves during performances what the differences are among different duologues (54).

The duologue assignment has several purposes. One is for the student to develop the ear. Another, related to the first, is to develop punctuation skills, a set of signals by the writer enabling the reader to reproduce as closely as possible the original voice. Moffett states, "Both transcribing and scripting offer excellent ways to learn punctuation through vocal intonation, a method that succeeds far better than conventional drills and rules" (54). The final purpose of the duologue is as a precomposition writing to get a student started, helping him or her to produce a great number of ideas to choose from later (55).

Duologues are an excellent workshop exercise; reading scripts aloud is the best way to see how to improve them. Two students sight-read through

a script cold, giving the author the chance to hear misreadings due to bad
punctuation, word choice, or misleading emphasis on sentence structure.
The class can then discuss the main effect that comes across. Questions to
ask are:

- Do the characters sound alike or different?
- Do they sound like the kind of person they are supposed to be? Or, from what
  they say and the way they say it, what kind of people are they?
- Does one dominate—bully or press the other one, initiate the topics?
- Describe what is happening between the speakers as they talk. Are they
  getting acquainted, plotting, scrapping, reassuring each other, avoiding some-
  thing, reminiscing, pleading, etc.?
- Where are they and what has brought them together?
- Have they known each other long? What is their relationship?
- Ask someone to draw two arrows on the board that represent their relationship—such as two arrows meeting head on, one pursuing the other, etc.
- Does the conversation have an end? If so, what brings on the end? Is it a slice
  or fragment?
- Pay close attention to the interaction between speakers, how well motivated
  their speeches are, and how much they create effects in each other. Are they
  really listening and reacting to each other, or are they talking somewhat
  independently?

If teachers need examples of duologues, Moffet (*Active Voice*) recom-
mends Saroyan's "Hello Out There," Kipling's "Danny Deever" and "Get
Up and Bar the Door," Yeats' "For Ann Gregory," Clark's "Streamside
Exchange," and Parker's "Telephone Conversation" (56).

Dialogue of Ideas

The students should use two voices, A and B, to discuss or argue some controversial issue. The discussion should be written in duologue form without stage
directions. Students can make up dialogue freely for about thirty minutes. This
can be performed by other students, printed, or used as a basis for further writing.

The main purpose of this exercise is to produce as many ideas about the
topic as possible, exploring all sides of an issue without the students feeling
compelled to build up a single case that avoids contradictions. The topic
may come from any other assignments, discussions, or readings. Often,
students who go blank when faced with the assignment, "Discuss the
following..." or who attempt to guess what the teacher wants to hear, may
be able to produce better and more honest ideas with this approach.
Another outcome of this exercise is that as an approach to exposition and

argumentation, it has the advantage of forcing the students to consider different sides of an issue, breaking down dogmatism and the simple one-sided point of view (65). In conjunction with this exercise, Moffet states that class discussion is very important as thinking is to a large extent an internalization of speech, of conversations one has had and heard (66). Thus, the external speaking through performance in this activity represents delivery.

Dialogue Converted to Essay

Have students rewrite their dialogues by merging the two voices into one without sacrificing any good ideas. They should feel free to add new ideas, get rid of weak ones, change words, and reorganize. Students may regard this edited version as a speech, editorial, or essay and follow up accordingly.

An important prerequisite of this activity is that students are naturally familiar with the topics of these dialogues and that the subjects do not require research or special experience. Topics should come out of the students' own efforts to think through issues they run into or from other work they are doing (*Active Voice* 68). Also important to this conversion is the crucial help students need with transitions in making smooth leaps from one idea to another or finding a concept that will harmonize the two or more viewpoints. Moffet believes that finding specialized words for the relationship of ideas is a logical matter that can be handled as they arise in particular cases instead of en bloc as a separate subject (69).

Another problem that might arise is organization. Several appropriate questions about organization to the student may help: Is the order of paragraphs interchangeable, or should there be some order in which they fall? Does the essay begin with the main assertions, which are then developed and illustrated, or are the main assertions in the conclusions? Which would be best? Is the same idea discussed in more than one place? Is it for a good reason, or just by chance?

Moffett has given us some very good suggestions on how to incorporate delivery in the writing or English classroom. His ideas seem to be a culmination of what I had in mind when I began to devise my theory of delivery. He begins with a simpler addition of voice, then adds the body, borrowing from the theater terms to fit these exercises. Thus, he weaves together a lesson plan for utilizing speaking, reading, listening, and writing in order to teach students how to better communicate. With his temporal order as an example, teachers can pick and choose the activities best suited to their students' needs.

Two Lesson Plans for Dramatizing Writing

I have shown how Moffett's model can give teachers a way of sequencing related activities for delivery in the classroom. In order to help teachers envision what specific lessons plans may look like, here I have provided two such plans. Both center on using delivery to reinforce audience awareness, but each employs different activities and approaches to public versus private writing.

Beginning writers often find it difficult to distinguish between public and private writing, or what Linda Flower calls "writer-based" and "reader-based" prose. That is, writer-based prose is a "verbal expression," written by, to, and for the writer, that reflects the associative action of the mind when verbally relating a topic. Such prose is typified by many references to the self, is loaded with code words (those known only to the writer), and is usually in a linear format. Reader-based prose, on the other hand, deliberately attempts to address an audience other than the self. It defines coded terms, refers less to the writer, and is structured around the topic. In its language and structure, reader-based prose reflects the purpose of the writer's thought, rather than its process as in writer-based prose (20).

As Flower states, writer-based prose, or private writing, is a first step to developing a polished work. Yet, without an understanding of such distinctions between this private and public discourse, students may transfer their prose straight onto the paper and believe it to be a completed essay. When asked to revise an essay to include a broader audience, the students cannot see those areas that need to be changed to perform such a feat. How can writing teachers harness this resource in the classroom? Where does delivery come in? The following two lesson plans make use of the delivery theory, giving teachers a way to help students improve writing skills through performance.

Plan One: Moving From Private to Public Writing

For Lesson Plan One, I have found that the dramatic monologue lends itself well to the writing classroom when teaching audience awareness and the movement from private to public writing. With thanks to Thomas Tyner and his textbook *Discovery* (St. Martin's Press, 1990), I have designed a unit that incorporates the writing of a dramatic monologue that is later rewritten into a narrative essay.

Class Day One

To prepare for this class, students are assigned to read three professionally written monologues taken from *A Pair of Jacks* by Lavonne Mueller, *Tim's Story* by James Pashalides (both from *Competition Monologues II*, 1989), *Out of Our Father's House* by Eve Merriam, Paula Wagner and Jack Hofsiss (*Competition Monologues*, 1988).

Class Activities: The students are divided into groups and asked to answer the following questions about each of the three monologues:

1. What experience is the speaker sharing with his or her audience?
2. Who is the audience of the monologue?
3. What is the purpose of the monologue?
4. What do we learn about the person speaking?
5. Who or what is the central figure in the monologue? What do we learn about the person or topic that the speaker is referring to?
6. What kind of description does the speaker use? Where is it used?
7. As the listener or reader, did you feel any kind of emotion during the monologue? If so, what and why?
8. What is your overall impression of the monologue?

After group discussion, the class is reassembled to share their answers and to come to some consensus of opinion. With this accomplished, the class then decides on the characteristics that make up an effective monologue, such as purpose, revelations about the speaker and a topic, use of description, a narrow audience, and so on.

Assignment for Next Time: Read the monologue "Painting Churches" by Tina Howe (1989) and answer the following questions:

1. What specific things did you like about the monologue? What did you find most interesting?
2. What questions did the monologue raise that you would like answered?
3. What is the purpose of the monologue?
4. What kind of description is used and where?
5. Thinking about the characteristics of an effective monologue, is there anything this monologue needs, is anything missing? If so, what?

Class Day Two

Class Activities: Discuss the students' answers, arriving at a consensus that the fourth monologue did or did not verify their characteristics of an effective monologue.

Hand out "Ideas for Monologues" and read through it in detail so students understand:

A monologue is a play, skit, or recitation which presents the words and/or thoughts of a single character. The passage can be in verse (like a poem) or it can be prose (like a piece of fiction), or it can combine these genres. Since you have already written one essay, you can think of a monologue as being almost like your first drafts—writer-based prose. A monologue, like an essay, has a specific audience, but here you have more freedom to choose an even more specific audience. Your monologue could be written to just one person, or to many, or to simply yourself (that would be an internal monologue). Remember the differences of approach to your writing when addressing various audiences. Keep that in mind as you choose your topic. Among other things, your mono- logue will be evaluated as to how well you can communicate with a certain narrow audience.

As for your topic for the monologue, you can choose one of those listed below, or you can also come up with your own. It is your choice. I simply thought giving you a list might help out some.

1. Describe your community (street, neighborhood, or town) and say why you live there or why you want to move.
2. Tell what happens in a day in the life of a typical suburban or urban wife, husband, son, or daughter.
3. Define yourself as a member of your family and show how you share values.
4. Choose a member of your family and describe him or her. What do you like about the person? What do you dislike? Is this person funny? Intelligent? What makes him or her unique?
5. Why did you come to Bowling Green State University (or college in general)?
6. What was the most embarrassing thing that has ever happened to you? (If choosing this, remember others will be reading or hearing it.)
7. What is the funniest thing that ever happened to you?
8. Describe the feeling you get on a roller coaster (or merry-go-round, airplane, train, toboggan, etc.).
9. My first day of high school (or gym, music lessons, swimming, babysitting, driving, using a computer, work, etc.)
10. My first writing assignment (or two-wheel bicycle, car, job, etc.).

Remind the students of what was discussed in class (what is a monologue and how is the audience involved), then provide topics to get them started. Some students may opt to choose a topic not on the list, something that I encourage, as doing so reinforces their interest in the monologue. They also must decide on their audience. Because these are to be specific and narrow, the majority of the students may choose to speak to one or two people, usually their close friends. In addition, while writing, the students are to keep in mind the characteristics of an effective monologue.

Divide students into groups and have them share their ideas for topics while other members of the group make suggestions and ask questions about the topic. Students take notes.

Assignment for Next Time: Come prepared to write in class. Have all your notes from the group session, a specific audience and topic in mind.

Class Day Three

Class Activities:
Students begin writing their monologues with help from group members and teacher when needed.

Assignment for Next Time: Finish the first draft of the monologue.

Class Day Four

Class Activities: Divide class into groups for peer revision. Each student acts out his or her monologue for other group members, with the teacher monitoring the progress from a distance. The authors first inform the group members who their audience is and the group must keep that in mind: how would that audience react to this monologue? After each performance, the writer/actor asks at least two questions about his or her monologue before group members begin discussion of the piece. The questions could pertain to anything, including how well the monologue was read or acted. Then the group is to answer the following questions:

1. What specific things did you like about the monologue? What did you find most interesting?
2. What questions did the monologue raise that you would like answered? Was there any information that was left out that you wanted to know about?
3. What do you think is the purpose of the monologue? Why might the author have chosen this subject as his or her monologue?
4. What audience is the monologue written for? Why do you think so?
5. What emotion does the monologue elicit? Should there be more? Where?
6. Who is the speaker; that is, what persona is used (i.e. young child, teen, old person, educated, etc.)? What is revealed about the speaker and where and how?
7. What is the topic of the monologue and what is revealed about it?
8. Where does the author make use of description? Would you like to see more description? If so, where?

The purpose of the peer questions is to help the students understand whether they are accomplishing what they set out to do with their monologues. If the responses they receive do not correspond with their monologue purpose, then they know they have to make revisions. Peers are also permitted to suggest what revisions should be made, or the students may see the teacher in conference for more guidance.

<u>Assignment for Next Time:</u>   Be ready to make revisions on the monologue in class. Have notes from peers ready.

Class Day Five

<u>Class Activities:</u>   Revise monologues with help from peers and from teacher.

<u>Assignment for Next Time:</u>   Finish revision of monologue and turn in for teacher comments. (Because I view these pieces as more of a stepping stone to the next piece of work, I grade them leniently, using Pass +, Pass, Pass –, based on whether students attempt to incorporate the characteristics of an effective monologue.)

Class Day Six

<u>Class Activities:</u>   As a whole class, use one of the professional monologues and turn it into a narrative. Remind students of the characteristics of an effective narrative essay, which should have been decided with their first essay of the term. (I realize this is an artificial exercise as they are not the original authors and I give them some leeway in incorporating some fabrication with the monologues.) Divide the class into peer groups and each group select one of the three remaining monologues and turn it into a narrative essay.

<u>Assignment for the Next Time:</u>   Complete today's assignment, turning monologue into narrative.

Class Day Seven

<u>Class Activities:</u>   Read narratives in class. After each reading, the group explains what steps were taken to make the transformation from monologue to narrative essay, and the class discusses whether or not the essay incorporated the characteristics of an effective narrative.

Assignment for Next Time: Be prepared to transform your own monologue into a narrative. Make notes on the things that you will need to change. Keep in mind the characteristics of an effective narrative essay and the steps we went through to rewrite the professional monologues.

Class Day Eight

Class Activities: Discuss at length audience awareness and why certain changes would have to occur in their monologues in order for them to appeal to a broader audience (such as the entire class or the whole student body), thus turning that private writing into public writing. To perform such a task, students usually decide they will have to change slang and expletives (if any), add transitions, develop some areas further, give more explanation, and so on. Then students transform their own monologues into narratives with help from peers and teacher.

Assignment for Next Time: Finish narrative and turn in for teacher comments.

Of course, assignments for this lesson plan may be compacted some or spread out more, depending on the length of particular classes. This plan has been successful in my developmental writing classes as well as introductory writing classes.

Furthermore, several aspects of the activities conform well with my theory of delivery. For instance, student ideas are transformed physically and delivered to the audience through the use of performance. With their monologues, the students convey their ideas to their peer audience and in reply, that audience, through discussion, delivers its response, be it good or bad.

Plan Two: Role-Playing in Peer Response

Lesson Plan Two (thanks to my colleague Priscilla Riggle) also tackles the problem of how to help students find a better way to locate the ever-elusive audience for their work. This plan, though, has less personal performance than the first but more collaborative work done through discussion.

Class Day One

Class Activities: Students receive two handouts: "Two Views of Audience" and "Writer-Based versus Reader-Based Prose" (see Appendix

A). I give a little background on the topic, referring them to the rubric that is used in the course. Then they read "Writer-Based versus Reader-Based Prose" and discuss it in their groups for the remaining time.

Assignment for Next Time: Read and write an informal two-page synthesized response to the two handouts.

Class Day Two

Class Activities: Students receive "Synthesis Paper" assignment (see Appendix A). Each student is assigned a writer role (the persona they will take on in writing the essay) and an audience (the intended readers for the essay). I will go over the guidelines—students then get into groups to begin composing biographies of the writer and audience roles. They will use the "Initial Group Meeting" and "Writer and Audience Roles" (see Appendix A) handouts to aid them in starting out. I encourage the students to improvise mannerisms and speech styles of each writer or audience role. One member should write or type the group's ideas.

Assignment for Next Time: Using the "Writer and Audience Roles" handout, brainstorm a list (as long as you can make it) of thoughts regarding your writer role and your assigned audience.

Class Day Three

Class Activities: Groups will finish composing a two-page biography of each writer or audience role, again improvising as they work.

Assignment for Next Time: Complete a rough draft of your essay and make copies for each group member.

Class Day Four

Class Activities: Each group member will take a turn reading his or her paper aloud. As they listen, the other two members play or act the audience for that writer and respond to the essay, based on their ideas of who the audience is.

Assignment for Next Time: Continue working on essays.

Class Day Five

Class Activities: The groups will finish reading and responding. They will work on revision if time allows.

Assignment for Next Time: Complete another draft and bring copies for the group.

Class Day Six

Class Activities: We will discuss as a class the issues and problems this assignment is raising. I will give a minilecture or discussion on the dangers of stereotyping. (For this, I enlist the help of students in acting out stereotypes as opposed to three-dimensional people.)

Assignment for Next Time: Each group member will use the minirubric (see Appendix A) to evaluate the other two papers.

Class Day Seven

Class Activities: Group members will return papers and discuss.

Assignment for Next Time: Revise based on either the rubrics or comments.

Class Day Eight

Class Activities: Individuals turn papers, with all notes and drafts attached, in to me. The whole class will share revisions and discuss changes and impressions of the assignment. When I comment on the essays, I will show how various aspects of the writing are tied to conceptions of audience.

As with the first lesson plan, this incorporates dramatizing writing throughout the process. First, we see it in the determining of writer and audience roles—just who are the people the students are writing to and what roles do they take as they write? By taking on these roles in improvisation and by implementing the theory of delivery, the students see the people actually come to life. The second area that uses physicality is the reading aloud of essays and the feedback of the peer groups acting as an audience. Finally, delivery is used when students and teacher demonstrate the dangers of stereotyping through a role-playing session.

CONCLUSION

In his article "Literacy in the Department of English," Jay Robinson writes, "I would suggest that a proper aim for introductory composition courses in the modern academy is to help students learn to play various roles that will lead to development of their minds, insofar as minds can usefully be shaped by the discourse and noetic systems of modern scholarship" (74). I agree that besides helping students to better their writing abilities, writing courses should better the minds of students. However, while extolling the mind, Robinson, like so many other theorists, seems to ignore the bodies of his students, something Whitehead in the 1920s warned against. Therefore, if we reincorporate delivery in the classroom along with the rest of the canon—invention, arrangement, style, and memory—we are admitting that our students have bodies and that physicality can be harnessed to improve their minds and their writing abilities.

Here, I want to repeat my delivery thesis: delivery in the writing classroom is the use of noetic and physical processes by which students can convey their ideas and life experiences to their peer audiences in an effort to develop the best writing they can achieve. As I have shown in this chapter, this can be accomplished through dramatizing writing, that is, by adding voice and body to students' writing efforts. By borrowing from the theater, teachers can easily give students the tools to incorporate their voices and bodies in every step of the writing process. From such simple assignments as reading aloud to one another, or stretching, to full improvised dramatic productions, students can give voice and body to their writing.

4

The Whole Restored With Delivery

In his most recent film, *Monster in a Box*, monologuist Spalding Grey recounts his first experience as a serious writer. He had gone to a writers' colony in New Hampshire where the writers, each given his or her own cottage, are left undisturbed throughout the day in order to devote their time to writing. Grey had gone there with great anticipation of being able to "really write." Instead of his usual sketchy notes for his mostly extemporaneous monologues, for which he is well known, he wanted to write his first book. Much to his chagrin, he had romanticized the writer's profession and discovered something ghastly: "It was horrible! I was left alone, only me, with my mind and hand working. Cooped up with only my mind and hand working. I developed huge calluses on my hand, while my brain just wanted to shut down" (paraphrased). Grey spent his weeks at the writers' colony in agony, not the ecstasy he had anticipated.

So it is with many students. They do not even anticipate the good life of writing. Instead, they simply dread the "horrible" task of writing alone, developing huge calluses while their brains shut down. For too long, students had a right to fear writing. Traditional classrooms were either silent or forbidding places where teachers lectured about grammar and style, then sent students off to complete essays on their own with no further guidance than an assigned topic—"In five pages argue for or against the World Bank," or "Research the Vietnam War and write twenty pages." Even in many contemporary classrooms, where teachers espouse the writing process, silence may still dominate while the students, mostly alone, scribble or tap out their ideas.

106

To break that silence, we must rejoin delivery to Cicero's four other canons—invention, arrangement, style, and memory. As I stated in the Introduction, in order to write effectively, students (or anyone) must have all steps in the process. If we fragment the whole, the rhetorical act inevitably suffers. As Kathleen Welch writes, the exclusion of delivery (and memory) from the five canons "undercuts the intentions and rhetorical fullness of the five-part structure" and "...ignores the orally based rhetoric that was the foundation of writing" (*Contemporary* 96–97). We must have what I call the sixth canon, the whole person, in order to have successful communication, written or spoken. By putting the "body," the physical act, back into writing, we have restored the whole. In order to perform this effort, I suggest that delivery be implemented through dramatizing writing, thus assisting students to move beyond that fear of writing in solitude. They can break the silence of the classroom and incorporate their entire bodies in the writing process.

However, I do not want to make it seem as if there has been absolutely no delivery in writing classes since the turn of the century. On the contrary, in more contemporary classrooms, teachers have utilized debates, discussions, role-playing, dramatic readings, and even some mime in order to motivate their students' ideas. What we have not had, though, is a theory underpinning these activities. Again, let me reiterate, teachers have followed theories on collaboration, audience, speaking, and writing. Even so, for the most part, writing theory has remained concerned with the minds and hands of students, not their bodies. With this text, I hope my theory of delivery has given teachers a theoretical framework for such practices and new ideas on how to implement the theory.

I must also say something about the teacher's role in this theory. Presently, teachers are guides in collaborative classes. In the classroom that incorporates delivery, we might describe teachers in some instances as directors. They give the assignment or directions, set the stage, and, finally, must let go to sit back to watch the performance. That assignment or direction is vastly important to the success of the production. Viola Spolin, teacher and author in drama education, states, "The director's energies must at all times be focused on finding, for both the actors and technical crews, deeper insights and perspectives to enhance the final theater communication" (*Theater Games* 9). In the writing classroom, we do not have actors and technical crews; we have students who are authors. All the same, our purpose is to "enhance the final... communication." Therefore, if the teacher's original assignment is not clear enough, then any failed communication cannot be the fault of the students. Teachers need to be thorough and concise in their assignments, or the dramatizing of writing will not be successful.

The purpose of this text has been to give teachers a theory behind the physical practices that currently exist in the classroom and to outline many more practical applications based on that theory. Hence, my work is divided into three main sections covering the history of delivery, facets of delivery that exist in current theory combined with my own theory of delivery, and practical applications of my theory.

In chapter 1, I have set up a continuum that travels from a totally physical delivery to a noetic delivery that incorporates more intellectual processes. Beginning with the sophists and moving through the Classical, Medieval, and Renaissance periods to the Elocutionary Movement, Neoclassical period and up to the rise of composition in the United States, I trace the movement of delivery back and forth along the continuum. My argument is that the tension heightened by discord over its definition eventually led to the splitting of delivery from the rhetorical canon. Theorists of written rhetoric claimed invention, arrangement, and style for their own and shunted memory and delivery to oral rhetoric. This division of the rhetorical canon remained in place so long that it encouraged a modern bias against delivery in writing. Nevertheless, delivery has once again come to the attention of writing theorists who also want to see a complete canon for the writing classroom.

In this chapter, I also include a separate discussion of women's challenge to delivery. Traditionally, women's speaking in public was frowned upon, if not forbidden. Therefore, theory about delivery has presumed a man speaking or delivering, a situation that has caused problems for researchers. Little literature exists on women in rhetoric, and those who are included make no mention of delivery in their theories. To overcome this lack of material, I re-visioned delivery in two forms so as to include women's voices in my work. I redefined women's "public" to include settings where women could speak, for example, behind-the-scenes maneuvering at palaces, as in the case of Pan Chao, a first century CE Chinese woman scholar; for later periods, I extrapolate a theory of delivery from spectators' descriptions of women delivering speeches, for instance, the tremendous energetic delivery of labor organizer Elizabeth Gurley Flynn.

Chapter 2 provides insight into the state of delivery in contemporary writing instruction. I argue that because the split of delivery from the rhetorical canon has caused a modern bias against delivery in writing theory, many strategies that could aid in the teaching of writing have either been overlooked or undertheorized. Therefore, I borrow from current theoretical areas within and outside of writing in order to construct my own theory of delivery. Included in my discussion of contemporary writing theory are sections on speaking and writing and dialogue (a combination of collaboration and audience). In addition, I cite performance theories from theater and some writing theorists who currently employ theater terminology, along with a discussion of feminist theories on "Writing the Body." My contention is that by integrating current writing theories with performance and writing the body, we can restore delivery to the rhetorical canon for writing. The chapter culminates in my own synthesized theory of delivery, incorporating facets from each of the chapter's divisions: delivery in the writing classroom is the use of noetic and physical processes by which students can convey their ideas and life experiences to their peer audiences in an effort to develop the best writing they can achieve. In order to implement this theory of delivery, I suggest that students "dramatize writing," borrowing activities and exercises from drama and other disciplines that incorporate physicality.

Practical applications of this theory is the topic of chapter 3. I believe that using drama as an implementation of delivery institutes a two-way communication through which writers and audiences learn from one another. In dramatizing writing, students employ both their physicality and their noetic processes, whether they are the writers or the audience. While employing delivery, teachers can reinstate the whole of the rhetorical canon throughout every step of the writing process. To facilitate its use, I divide this chapter according to the type of physicality or performance that is most dominant in each activity. In "Dramatizing Voice Alone," I include exercises that use only the voice, for instance, reading essays aloud to peers or reading the essay into a tape recorder for the teacher's comments, which are also recorded. The second section, "Dramatizing Body Alone," covers body movements that do not use the voice. For example, the students can develop tableaux to symbolize the topics they are working on, or they can choose an emotion to mime. Thirdly, "Full Physical Performance" highlights activities in which the students use both voice and movement more equally, as with improvisation or interviewing. This section is further subdivided by several categories: improvisation, role-playing, word play, interviewing, meetings, documentary, talk–write, and miscellaneous delivery. For each category, I describe several activities, state how they fit with delivery, and when during the process of writing they can be utilized.

To further aid teachers in employing delivery throughout the writing process, I have also included in the chapter a summary of James Moffett's strategies that employ my interpretation of dramatizing writing in a step-by-step process for the classroom, followed by two specific lesson plans that outline the use of dramatizing writing for an essay assignment.

Thus far, I have traced delivery through rhetorical history, discussed the theories that impact my own new theory of delivery, and shown teachers many ways in which to apply this theory. Ultimately, my purpose has been to give teachers new and more strategies to aid them in the teaching of writing. Still, this is only a small part of what needs to be done in this field of writing theory. Many other areas require extensive research.

First, one aspect of delivery that I did not touch on in my text is the connection between delivery and "ethos," the speaker's authority, or how the audience perceives the speaker. According to Aristotle, ethical appeal can be the most effective kind of appeal; even the most clever and most sound appeal to reason could fall on deaf ears if the audience reacted unfavorably to the speaker's character. The whole discourse must maintain the image that the writer seeks to establish. The effect of ethical appeal might be destroyed by a single lapse from good sense, goodwill, or moral integrity. Of course, Aristotle was concerned with oral rhetoric, but how does his ethos impact delivery in the writing classroom? Does my theory of delivery change in relation to a concern for ethos? Where does ethos fit into dramatizing writing?

Second, I ignored the rhetorical element of memory while espousing the rejoining of delivery to Cicero's five parts of the successful speech. Of course, we would still be without the whole if we left out one facet. Memory is just as important to the success of writing as is delivery and the other elements of the rhetorical canon. Therefore, memory, too, needs to be examined in relationship to contemporary writing classes: Where does memory fit in with the history of rhetoric? What is its impact on invention, arrangement, style, and delivery? What is memory's function in the success of writing? Has that function changed over time? Can we design a new theory of memory? How can teachers better incorporate memory in their classrooms?

A third area ripe for exploration is the division between writing and speaking that took place at the turn of the century. Despite the fact that some rhetoricians still held that writing and speaking were necessarily connected, the overwhelming majority of teachers at that time divided oral and written communication. As I wrote before, invention, arrangement, and style were relegated to written discourse, and memory and delivery were sent to oral rhetoric. This division of Cicero's canons also heralded the separation of rhetoric into English and speech departments. Questions to answer for this topic could include: how did the separation of the written component affect the oral component of rhetoric, and vice versa? Why did the "oral composition" espoused by overworked composition teachers never catch on? In what ways did the students' writing suffer from the lack of speech in the composition classroom at that time?

Of course, as in so many other disciplines, women's roles in rhetoric and writing need more investigation. In order for this to occur, though, digging for lost manuscripts and texts by women is imperative. Women are sadly underrepresented in the rhetorical field, although that is slowly and painfully being corrected. Some questions that might be asked here are: were there any women rhetoricians who espoused a theory of delivery or who even adhered to Cicero's canon? In what ways did the rhetoric classroom before the separation of speaking and writing differ for women as compared to men? Are there inherent differences in how women speak and write as compared to men? Some theorists claim there is a feminine and masculine style of writing; does that hold true for delivery? Before modern times, was there ever a time, place, or reason where women were free to speak publicly? If so, how was that accomplished?

Furthermore, an area greatly wanting research is the other marginalized voices besides women that have been ignored for so long, those of people of color and of non-European people. Like women, manuscripts and texts for these voices are also hard to come by. They have been lost, destroyed, or simply not yet uncovered. However, many of the questions unanswered about women's speaking and writing are still not answered for these people: How would delivery for marginalized peoples differ from that of White Western males? Did these groups have any theories and ideas similar to Cicero's canon? How would their work fit into the categories of invention, arrangement, style, memory, and delivery? Unfortunately, we may never know the answers.

Besides these many areas that have yet to be investigated, I am sure there must still be a myriad of unanswered questions in the field of oral and written communication, particularly questions as to how to give the necessary tools to our students in order to better their writing abilities. In this text, I have simply touched on an area that can afford teachers ways in which to give students those tools, but more needs to be done.

Delivery in the classroom through dramatizing writing aids students to use their bodies and minds in their writing. With delivery, students can, with the help of others, study themselves, hear themselves, and see themselves as users of language. They will not need to discover how horrible writing alone can be, using only their brains and calloused hands; they will have the advantage over Spalding Grey.

Appendix A

Lesson Plan Two Handouts

The following are the various handouts needed for Lesson Plan Two:

TWO VIEWS OF AUDIENCE

At some point in your writing careers, you have probably all heard the word "audience." Some of you may have even had such comments as "consider your audience" marked on your papers. What is audience? How do you "consider" it? For the sake of simplicity, I will limit our class discussions for the most part to two general views of audience: I will refer to them as the *classical* and the *imagined* approaches.

The classical approach usually emphasizes the thorough analysis of the audience so that the writer may persuade the readers to think or act a certain way. For example, a writer composing an editorial to the *BG News* is trying to persuade the administration and the English department to change English 112 to a year-long course. The writer might try to anticipate the audience's probable response and figure out the best way to write the editorial to obtain the desired response. Traditionally, the writer who subscribes to the classical view has a persuasive task at hand and is dealing with a potentially hostile audience.

A less-structured way of looking at audience is the imagined approach. Such a view does not assume that we know who our audience is when we write; therefore, a formal analysis is not possible. The writer in this second situation must somehow find or represent the audience in his or her imagination. If this sounds complicated, it usually is until the imagination becomes trained to automatically seek out the audience for a piece of writing. When the writer has found a reader or group of readers, he or she must then make clear in the written work who the audience is supposed to be.

There are many points in between these two views, and we can discuss various other approaches and integrations of approaches as we work on the assignment. For now, I'd like you to think about what you usually do when you write. Do you think it would make a difference in your writing to think about who your audience is before and as you work? Do you usually think about your audience when you write? If so, is the audience generally your teacher or classmates? Because we will be spending the next few weeks working on audience awareness, you should begin to find where you stand on the topic—and we'll take it from there.

WRITER-BASED VERSUS READER-BASED PROSE[1]

You have to wonder why it is so difficult sometimes to say what you mean when you write! There are probably many explanations for the problem, but one that makes particularly good sense to me is this: when we write as a way of communicating with others, we can't just record our thoughts directly from the brain to the paper in front of us. If we are writing for ourselves, such as making a list or entering thoughts into a diary, we know we will be able to go back and usually understand what we meant. We also know that if someone else picked up either of these pieces of writing, the reader might not understand exactly what we meant.

Therein lies the problem. Unfortunately, many of us, even when we intend our writing to be read by others, are still writing as if we are composing a list or writing in a private diary. We may rely heavily on narrative and use few details or connectors. This kind of writing is egocentric, that is, self-centered. We might as well have written it for ourselves, because no one else can understand exactly what we meant. Our words only have meaning to us. This is what we call *writer-based prose*.

Rough drafts are usually writer-based prose. The thought processes are translated into the writing process, and a person who picks up that draft sees words that are still under construction. There is nothing wrong with a rough draft that looks like this, but this piece of writing will have to undergo radical revision before it is reader based.

---

[1]This is a summary of an essay by Linda Flower entitled "Writer-Based Prose: A Cognitive Basis for Problems in Writing." You can find the full essay in *College English*, Sept. 1979, pages 19+.

Reader-based prose is exactly the opposite of writer-based prose. Whether the writer uses the word "you" or not, this kind of writing is clearly intended for someone else to read. A reader-based essay is a joy to read because you feel as if the writer took you and your needs into consideration every step of the way. With a little time and a lot of distance from our writing, we can all learn to translate our inner thoughts into words that can reach others. When we do, we will discover what makes writing fun, fulfilling, and purposeful, which is knowing there is a place where the writer and reader of a work can meet—and that is inside the work itself.

SYNTHESIS PAPER ASSIGNMENT

Topic. Using your assigned writing role and audience, describe, in about three pages, how members of your audience might make use of humor in their lives, jobs, etc. The controlling purpose of the essay is to convince this group of people that humor has value for them for very specific reasons. You will need to use at least one of the theories of humor from your *Writing and Reading Across the Curriculum* (Behrens and Rosen 1997) chapter to explain your ideas. Use the guidelines on the inside front cover of the text to write your essay.

Your writing role and audience are circled below:

Writing Roles	Audience
Parent of young children	Parents of young children
A college student	College students
A college professors	College professors
	An adolescent going through puberty

INITIAL GROUP MEETING

1. Discuss the writer and audience roles in any order that you wish—but decide on an order right away. Have one group member write or type ideas you discuss.
2. You might try to speak in general first, then see how the assignment requirements and the writer and audience roles intersect.
3. Feel free to discuss the differences among the four groups of people; also, you might think about and reflect upon how this is different from writing to the teacher.

4. You will use the ideas you come up with in this meeting to write your paper and to reflect on each other's papers as you work together.

WRITING AND AUDIENCE ROLES

These are prompts to help you begin to visualize four groups of people—use them as an aid, but feel free to take off on your own. Stereotyping is probably inevitable, so be aware of that as you work, and we will discuss the implication at a later date.

- What, in general, do I think of when I think of this group of people?
- What are these people like?
- How old are they likely to be? In what ways might their ages affect their needs/expectations?
- What tone of voice would I probably use or what attitude would I want to project when talking with this group of people?
- Is this group likely to readily accept what I have to say to them? Why or why not?
- What are their educational experiences especially with regard to types/levels of writing?
- What interests, values, attitudes, and so on, do I share with these people?

AUDIENCE MINIRUBRIC

Make checks next to the areas where you feel more attention is needed to audience. Please make extensive comments on a separate sheet of paper.

____ credibility of information or argument
____ tone
____ point of view (both verb tense and pronoun usage)
____ clarity of thesis
____ type of organizational pattern
____ kinds of and numbers of examples or illustrations
____ types of sentences (length, style, etc.)
____ kinds of and levels of words used
____ grammar, usage, mechanics

Appendix B

Examples for Role-Playing

The following are examples of scenarios and role cards for the role-playing activity in chapter 3 (taken from Rubin and Dodd 13–14).

Dilemma: Should the drinking age be lowered?
Scene: Seated in the bleachers, waiting for professional baseball game to begin.

(Four roles—to be placed on individual index cards. Opening dialogue may also accompany the descriptions.)

Paul: 18-year-old college student who works summers at the local golf course

Mary: mother of high school daughter; she works as a teacher

If I'm old enough to be drafted, to vote, or be married, then why shouldn't I have the privilege of drinking? I can go out and die for my country, but I can't drink.

Kids today just want to party all the time, and they don't think of the consequences involved. My sister's child was hit by a college student on his way home from a party. I don't want to see that happen to my child.

Greg: 40-year-old bar owner who's been divorced and has three children

Lisa: 30-year-old physician who practices in a college town

They've really hurt my business raising the drinking age from 18 to 21. It's just a small business, and college students are my biggest customers. I really need the extra business that would come in if they lowered the age.

Alcohol is a dangerous drug. I have treated too many young people who have abused it, or who have been injured because others have abused it.

Of course, teachers may add or subtract from these samples. For more such examples, see Rubin and Dodd's *Talking into Writing* (Urbana: NCTE, 1987).

Appendix C

Types of Roles for Debate

The following is the list of types of arguments and types of roles (Rubin and Dodd 47–48) used in the debate activity from chapter 3:

TYPES OF ARGUMENTS

1. <u>Cause and Effect:</u> Something is the cause of something else. If we observe an effect, we can be pretty sure that the cause is responsible. If we observe the cause, we can be pretty sure that the effect will follow.

   Example: If we legalize marijuana, more people will become hooked on hard drugs because smoking marijuana causes people to try hard drugs. After all, once you've broken one law against drug use, it's easy to break another. Also, marijuana gives us bad judgment, so it's harder to resist the temptation of hard drugs.

2. <u>Example:</u> What is true in a particular example(s) is true in general.

   Example If more people use marijuana, we will see more tragic deaths from drug overdoses. After all, Jimi Hendrix, Janis Joplin, and John Belushi all died from drug-related causes.

3. <u>Analogy:</u> What is true in one case will be true in another case that is similar.

   Example: We should legalize marijuana because we are just wasting money trying to prohibit it; we'll never be successful in wiping it out. After all, think about the period during the 1920s when alcoholic beverages were prohibited. The government eventually had to return to allowing consumption of alcohol because Prohibition simply wasn't working.

4. <u>Sign:</u> When two things usually occur together, if we observe one of those things, we can be pretty sure that the other exists.

   Example: When we allow marijuana use to go unchecked, we are allowing our civilization to fall apart. Whenever large numbers of people pursue pleasure that has no constructive effect, that's a sure sign that civilization is going downhill.

5. <u>Authority:</u> If an expert in a certain area says something, it's probably true.

   Example: The district attorney of Blue Earth County agrees that we should legalize marijuana. She has prosecuted a large number of cases involving marijuana possession, and she concludes that these court cases are a waste of the taxpayers' money.

ROLES OF ARGUMENTS IN DEBATES

Supporting the new proposal: If you are supporting the new policy or issue, you must show three things:

1. <u>Need:</u> There is a problem, and the existing policy does not solve it.

   Example: Drug smuggling is a major problem in the United States. Many violent crimes are committed by criminals engaged in drug smuggling. Stiff laws that make possession of marijuana illegal are not stopping the drug smugglers.

2. <u>Solution:</u> The new policy would help to solve the problem.

   Example: If marijuana were no longer illegal, then bringing it into the United States would no longer be a criminal activity. Legitimate businesses would take over, and violent criminals would no longer be involved.

3. <u>Practicality:</u> The new policy can be implemented and would not create new problems that might be just as troubling.

   Example: It would take a simple act of Congress to legalize marijuana. So many people use marijuana now that there probably wouldn't be much increase in usage. Besides, even if more people did use marijuana, the situation wouldn't be as bad as all the drunk drivers on the road who use alcohol.

Attacking the new proposal (supporting the existing policy): If you are attacking the new policy and defending the policy which already exists, you must show three things:

1. <u>No Need:</u> The existing policy does a good job of controlling the problem.

   Example: The existing laws which make marijuana illegal have a powerful effect. These laws keep most youngsters from running around intoxicated all the time. Most youngsters who do use marijuana use it sparingly because it is pretty expensive, and they are also afraid of getting into trouble with the law.

2. <u>New Policy Wouldn't Work:</u> Even if there were a big problem, the proposed policy wouldn't solve it.

   Example: Even if marijuana were legalized, we would still have the most dangerous kind of drug smuggling. Highly addictive drugs such as cocaine and heroin would still attract the most violent criminals.

3. <u>New Policy Would Create Problems:</u> If we adopted the proposed policy, we would face a whole new set of serious problems.

   Example: If marijuana were legalized, we certainly wouldn't allow young kids to use it, any more than we allow young kids to drink alcohol. We would need a whole new set of regulations and a whole new set of police procedures to make sure that young kids don't get hold of marijuana. Keeping alcohol out of their hands is enough of a problem. Why add another one?

Appendix D

"Happening" Activities

The following are examples of the activities Lutz had his students perform during his first "Happening" (37):

Go to the front of the room and face the class. Count to yourself and each time you reach five say, "If I had the wings of an angel."

Go to the front right corner of the room and hide your head in it. Keep counting to yourself and on every third number say loudly, "Home."

Sit in your seat and watch the person facing you from the front of the room. Each time he/she says "Angel" you clap. Don't look anywhere else.

Be an ice cream cone—change flavor.

Look at your feet but don't ever move them or look up or anywhere else in the room.

Gently tap your forehead against your desk. Keep doing this without looking around.

Walk around to everyone in the room and pat him/her on the back lightly and say "It's all right." Stop occasionally and say "Who, me?" (37)

References

Adams, John Quincy. *Lectures on Rhetoric and Oratory*. Cambridge, MA: Hilliard and Metcalf, 1810. New York: Russell and Russell, 1962.

Allen, R. R. "The Rhetoric of John Franklin Genung." *Speech Teacher* 12 (1963): 238–41.

Anderson, Dorothy I. "Edward T. Channing's Definition of Rhetoric." *Speech Monographs* 14 (1947): 81–92.

Aristotle. *The Rhetoric and the Poetics of Aristotle*, ed. Ingram Bywater. New York: Random House, 1984.

Astell, Mary. *A Serious Proposal to the Ladies for the Advancement of their True and Greatest Interest*. 1701. 4th ed. New York: Source Book, 1970.

Augustine, Dorothy, and W. Ross Winterowd. "Speech Acts and the Reader-Writer Transaction." *Convergences: Transactions in Reading and Writing*, ed. Bruce T. Petersen. Urbana: NCTE, 1986. 127–48.

Austin, Gilbert. *Chironomia; or A Treatise on Rhetorical Delivery*, eds. Margaret Robb and Lester Thonssen. Carbondale: Southern Illinois UP, 1966.

Bacon, Francis. "The Advancement of Learning." *The Rhetorical Tradition*, eds. Patricia Bizzell and Bruce Herzberg. Boston: St. Martin's, 1990. 625–31.

– – –. *On Communication and Rhetoric*, ed. Karl R. Wallace. Raleigh: University of North Carolina Press, 1943.

Barthes, Roland. *The Pleasure of the Text*, trans. Richard Miller. New York: Hill and Wang, 1975.

Bartholomae, David. "The Study of Error." *Rhetoric and Composition*, ed. Richard L. Graves. Upper Montclair: Boynton, 1984. 311–27.

Behrens, Laurence, and Leonard Rosen. *Writing and Reading Across the Curriculum*. New York: Longman, 1997.

Berlin, James. *Writing Instruction in Nineteenth Century Colleges*. Southern Illinois UP, 1984.

Bernhardt, Stephen A. "Visual Rhetoric." *Encyclopedia of Rhetoric and Composition*, ed. Theresa Enos. New York: Garland, 1996. 746–48.

Bizzell, Patricia, and Bruce Herzberg. *The Rhetorical Tradition*. Boston: St. Martin's, 1990.

Braxandall, Rosalyn Fraad. *Words on Fire*. New Brunswick: Rutgers UP, 1987.

Brooke, Robert, et al. *Small Groups in Writing Workshops: Invitations to a Writer's Life*. Urbana: NCTE, 1994.

Brooke, Robert E. *Writing and Sense of Self*. Urbana: NCTE, 1991.

Brookes, Gerald. "'Town Meetings': A Strategy for Including Speaking in a Writing Classroom." *College Composition and Communication* 44.1 (February 1993): 88–92.

Bruffee, Kenneth A. "Collaboration and the 'Conversation of Mankind'." *College English* 46 (1984): 635–52.

Buck, Gertrude. *A Course in Argumentative Writing.* New York: Holt, 1901.

Burke, Kenneth. *A Grammar of Motives.* New York: Prentice-Hall, 1952.

Campbell, Karlyn Kohrs. *Man Cannot Speak for Her.* Vol. 1 & 2. New York: Praeger, 1989.

Casaregola, Vincent, and Julie Farrar. "Twentieth-Century Rhetoric." *Encyclopedia of Rhetoric and Composition,* ed. Theresa Enos. New York: Garland, 1996. 732–39.

Chapman, Gerald. *Teaching Young Playwrights.* Portsmouth: Heinemann, 1991.

Cicero. *De Inventione.* London: Harvard UP, 1949.

– – –. *Of Oratory.* Carbondale: Southern Illinois UP, 1970.

– – –. "From *Of Oratory.*" *The Rhetorical Tradition,* eds. Patricia Bizzell and Bruce Herzberg. Boston: St. Martin's, 1990. 200–50.

– – –. *Orator.* Cambridge: Harvard UP, 1952.

Cixous, Helene. "The Laugh of the Medusa." *Signs* 1 (Summer 1976): 245–64.

Collins, James L. "Speaking, Writing, and Teaching for Meaning." *Exploring Speaking–Writing Relationships,* eds. Barry M. Kroll and Robert J. Vann. Urbana: NCTE, 1981. 198–214.

Comprone, Joseph. "Kenneth Burke and the Teaching of Writing." *College Composition and Communication* 29 (December 1978): 336–40.

Connors, Robert. "Actio: A Rhetoric of Written Delivery (Iteration Two)." *Rhetorical Memory and Delivery,* ed. John Frederick Reynolds. Hillsdale: Lawrence Erlbaum Associates, 1993. 65–77.

– – –. "Greek Rhetoric and the Transition From Orality." *Philosophy and Rhetoric* 19 (1986): 38–65.

Connors, Robert, Lisa Ede, and Andrea Lunsford. *Essays on Classical Rhetoric and Modern Discourse.* Carbondale: Southern Illinois UP, 1984.

Day, Henry. "The Art of Discourse." *The Rhetorical Tradition,* eds. Patricia Bizzell and Bruce Herzberg. Boston: St. Martin's, 1990. 864–73.

de Pizan, Christine. *A Medieval Woman's Mirror of Honor: The Treasury of the City of Ladies.* New York: Persea, 1989.

Donlan, Dan. *Teachers as Playwrights: Problems of Form, Voice, and Audience.* ERIC ED 239310. 1983.

Dragga, Sam. "The Ethics of Delivery." *Rhetorical Memory and Delivery,* ed. John Frederick Reynolds. Hillsdale: Lawrence Erlbaum Associates, 1993. 79–95.

Elbow, Peter. *Teacher Writing Without Teachers.* New York: Oxford UP, 1973.

Emig, Janet. *The Composing Processes of Twelfth Graders.* Urbana: NCTE, 1971.

Ettlich, Ernest Earl. "John Franklin Genung and the Nineteenth Century Definition of Rhetoric." *Central States Speech Journal* 17 (1966): 283–88.

Faules, Don. "Joseph Villiers Denney: English Scholar and Contributor in the Emergence of Speech Theory." *Speech Teacher* 12 (1963): 105–9.

Fleming, Margaret. "Getting Out of the Writing Vacuum." *Focus on Collaboration.* Urbana: NCTE, 1988. 77–84.

Flower, Linda. "Writer-Based Prose: A Cognitive Basis for Problems in Writing." *College English* 41 (September, 1979): 19–37.

Friday, Robert A., and Bernard F. Beranek. *Report on a Pilot Which Combined Speech Communication and English Composition Instruction.* ERIC ED 279046. 1987.

Gere, Ann Ruggles. *Writing Groups: History, Theory, and Implications.* Carbondale: Southern Illinois UP, 1987.

Gilbertsen, Michael, and M. Jimmie Killingsworth. "Behavioral Talk–Write as a Method for Teaching Technical Editing." *Iowa State Journal of Business and Technical Communication* 1 (1987): 108–14.

Gill, Glenda E. "The African-American Student: At Risk." *College Composition and Communication* 43.2 (May 1992): 225–30.

Golden, James L. "Plato Revisited: A Theory of Discourse for All Seasons." *Essays on Classical Rhetoric and Modern Discourse*, eds. Robert Connors, Andrea Lunsford, and Lisa Ede, Carbondale: Southern Illinois UP, 1984. 16–36.

Guthrie, Warren. "The Development of Rhetorical Theory in America 1635–1850." *Speech Monographs* 14 (1947): 45.

– – –. "Rhetorical Theory in Colonial America." *History of Speech Education in America: Background Studies*, ed. Karl E. Wallace. New York: Appleton, 1954, 45–51.

Hagaman, John A. "'Readiness is All': The Importance of Speaking and Writing Connections." *Journal of Teaching Writing* 5.2 (Fall 1986): 187–92.

Halpern, Jeanne. "Differences Between Speaking and Writing and Their Implications for Teaching." *College Composition and Communication* 35 (1984): 345–57.

Hatch, Gary Layne, and Margaret Bennett Walters. "Robert Zoellner's Talk–Write Pedagogy." *Writing Ourselves into the Story*, eds. Sheryl I. Fontaine and Susan Hunter. Carbondale: Southern Illinois UP, 1993. 335–51.

Heathcote, Dorothy. *Dorothy Heathcote: Collected Writings on Education and Drama*, eds. Liz Johnson and Cecily O'Neill. London: Hutchinson, 1984.

Helsley, Sheri L. "A Special Afterword to Graduate Students." *Rhetorical Memory and Delivery*, ed. John Frederick Reynolds. Hillsdale: Lawrence Erlbaum Associates, 1993. 157–59.

Hill, David J. *Science of Rhetoric*. New York: Sheldon, 1877.

Hogg, Mary. *Creative Dramatics and the Elderly*. Paper presented at the Annual Meeting of the Speech Communication Association, November 18–21, 1989. ERIC ED 315815. 1989.

Howell, Wilbur Samuel. *Eighteenth-Century British Logic and Rhetoric*. Princeton: Princeton UP, 1971.

– – –. "English Backgrounds of Rhetoric." *History of Speech Education in America: Background Studies*, ed. Karl E. Wallace. New York: Appleton, 1954.

– – –, ed. *Fenelon's Dialogues on Eloquence*. Princeton: Princeton UP, 1951.

– – –. *Logic and Rhetoric in England, 1500–1700*. New York: Russell and Russell, 1961.

Johannesen, Richard L. "The Emerging Concept of Communication as Dialogue." *Quarterly Journal of Speech* 57 (1971): 373–82.

Johnson, Harriet Hall. "Margaret Fuller as Known by Her Scholars." *Christian Register* (April 21, 1910): 427–29. *Critical Essays on Margaret Fuller*, ed. Joel Myerson. Boston: G.K. Hall, 1980. 134–40.

Johnson, Nan. *Nineteenth-Century Rhetoric in North America*. Carbondale: Southern Illinois UP, 1991.

Jones, Ann Rosalind. "Writing the Body: Toward an Understanding of l'Ecriture Feminine." *Feminist Criticism and Social Change*, eds. J. Newton and D. Rosenfelt. New York: Methuen, 1985. 85–101.

Josipovici, Gabriel. *Writing and the Body*. Princeton: Princeton UP, 1982.

Keith, Philip. "Re-examination of George Yoos' 'Role-Identity in Reading and Writing.'" *Rhetorical Society Quarterly* 20.4 (Fall, 1990): 357–60.

Kennedy, George. *The Art of Persuasion in Greece*. Princeton: Princeton UP, 1963.

– – –. *Classical Rhetoric and Its Christian and Secular Tradition from Ancient to Modern Times*. Chapel Hill: University of North Carolina Press, 1980.

Kitzhaber, Albert R. *Rhetoric in American Colleges, 1850–1900*. Arlington: Methodist UP, 1989.

Knabe, Jason D. "Creative Dramatics and Oral Interpretation in the Composing Process." *Teachers and Writers: Articles from the Ohio Writing Project*, ed. Mary Hayes. ERIC ED 232210. 1981.

Kolodny, Annette. "Margaret Fuller: Inventing a Feminist Discourse." *Reclaiming Rhetorica: Women in the Rhetorical Tradition*, ed. Andrea A. Lunsford. Pittsburgh: University of Pittsburgh Press, 1995. 137–66.

Kroll, Barry M. "Developmental Relationships between Speaking and Writing." *Exploring Speaking–Writing Relationships*, eds. Barry M. Kroll and Robert J. Vann. Urbana: NCTE, 1981. 32–54.

LeFevre, Karen Burke. *Invention as a Social Act*. Carbondale: Southern Illinois UP, 1987.

Lutz, William D. "Making Freshman English a Happening." *College Composition and Communication* 22 (1971): 35–38.

McCaslin, Nellie. *Creative Drama in the Classroom*. New York: Longman, 1990.

Meyers, George Douglas. "Adapting Zoellner's 'Talk–Write' to the Business Writing Classroom." *Bulletin of the Association for Business Communication* 48 (1985): 14–16.

Minh-ha, Trinh T. *Woman, Native, Other*. Bloomington: Indiana UP, 1989.

Moffett, James. *Active Voice: A Writing Program Across the Curriculum*. Upper Montclair: Boynton, 1981.

– – –. *Drama: What is Happening*. Champaign: NCTE, 1967.

– – –. *Teaching the Universe of Discourse*. Boston: Houghton Mifflin, 1968.

Morgan, Norah, and Juliana Saxton. *Teaching Drama*. London: Hutchinson, 1987.

Murphy, James J., ed. *Rhetoric in the Middle Ages: A History of Rhetorical Theory from Saint Augustine to the Renaissance*. Berkeley: University of California Press, 1974.

– – –, ed. *A Short History of Writing Instruction*. Davis: Hermagoras, 1990.

– – –. *A Synoptic History of Classical Rhetoric*. Davis: Hermagoras, 1983.

Neelands, Jonathan. *Making Sense of Drama: A Guide to Classroom Practice*, 4th ed. Oxford: Heinemann, 1989.

Ochsner, Robert S. *Physical Eloquence and the Biology of Writing*. SUNY Press, 1990.

Ong, Walter. "Literacy and Orality in Our Times." *Composition and Literature: Bridging the Gap*, ed. Winifred Horner. Chicago: University of Chicago Press, 1983. 84–96.

Pan Chao. *Lessons for Women*. trans. Nancy Lee Swann. In *Pan Chao: Foremost Woman Scholar of China, First Century A. D.* 1932. New York: Russell and Russell, 1968.

Pfister, Fred R., and Joanne F. Petrick. "A Heuristic Model for Creating a Writer's Audience." *College Composition and Communication* 30 (May 1980): 213–14.

Quintilian. "Institutes of Oratory." *The Rhetorical Tradition*, eds. Patricia Bizzell and Bruce Herzberg. Boston: St. Martin's, 1990. 297–363.

– – –. *Institutio Oratoria*. trans. H. E. Butler. New York: Loeb Classical Library, 1921.

Radcliffe, Terry. "Talk–Write Composition: A Rhetorical Model Proposing the Use of Speech to Improve Writing." *Research in the Teaching of English* 6 (1972): 187–99.

Rahskopf, Horace G. "John Quincy Adams: Speaker and Rhetorician." *Quarterly Journal of Speech* 32 (1946): 435–41.

Reynolds, John Frederick. "Delivery." *Encyclopedia of Rhetoric and Composition*, ed. Theresa Enos. New York: Garland, 1996. 172–73.

– – –, ed. *Rhetorical Memory and Delivery*. Hillsdale: Lawrence Erlbaum Associates, 1993.

Richardson, Marilyn, ed. *Maria W. Stewart, America's First Black Woman Political Writer*. Bloomington: Indiana UP, 1987.

Robb, Mary Margaret. *Oral Interpretation of Literature in American Colleges and Universities*. New York: Wilson, 1941.

Robinson, Jay L. "Literacy in the Department of English." *The Writing Teacher's Sourcebook*, eds. Gary Tate and Edward P. J. Corbett. Oxford: Oxford UP, 1981. 65–81.

Rubin, Donald L., and William M. Dodd. *Talking into Writing*. Urbana: NCTE, 1987.

Sabio, David. "Actio." *Encyclopedia of Rhetoric and Composition*, ed. Theresa Enos. New York: Garland, 1996. 1–2.

Schafer, John C. "The Linguistic Analysis of Spoken and Written Texts." *Exploring Speaking–Writing Relationships*, eds. Barry M. Kroll and Robert J. Vann. Urbana: NCTE, 1981. 1–31.

Schneir, Mirian, ed. *Feminism: The Essential Historical Writings*. New York: Vintage, 1972.

Sheridan, Thomas. *A Course of Lectures on Elocution*. Dublin: Samuel Whyte, 1762.

– – –. "A Course of Lectures on Elocution, Lecture VI." *The Rhetorical Tradition*, eds. Patricia Bizzell and Bruce Herzberg. Boston: St. Martin's, 1990. 730–37.

Smagorinsky, Peter. "The Aware Audience." *English Journal* 80.5 (September, 1991): 35–40.

Smail, William M. *Quintilian on Education*. Oxford: Clarendon Press, 1938.

Sommers, Jeffrey. "The Effects of Tape-Recorded Commentary on Student Revision: A Case Study." *Journal of Teaching Writing* 8.2 (Fall/Winter 1989): 49–75.

Sommers, Nancy. "Responding to Student Writing." *College Composition and Communication*, 33 (1982) 148–56.

Spolin, Viola. *Improvisation for the Theatre*. Evanston: Northwestern UP, 1983.

– – –. *Theater Games for Rehearsal*. Evanston: Northwestern UP, 1985.

Stebbins, Genevieve. *Delsarte System of Dramatic Expression*. New York: E. S. Werner, 1886. 6th enlarged ed. 1902. New York: Dance Horizon, 1977.

Stewart, Donald C. "The Nineteenth Century." *The Present State of Scholarship in Historical and Contemporary Rhetoric*, ed. Winifred Bryan Horner. Columbia: University of Missouri, 1983.

Swartz, Larry. *Dramathemes: A Practical Guide for Teaching Drama*. Ontario: Pembroke, 1988.

Tyner, Thomas. *Discovery*. Boston: St. Martin's, 1990.

Wallace, Karl E., ed. *History of Speech Education in America: Background Studies*. New York: Appleton, 1954.

Ward, John. *A System of Oratory*. London: Cornhill, 1759.

Watkins, Brian. *Drama and Education*. London: Batsford, 1981.

Welch, Kathleen. *The Contemporary Reception of Classical Rhetoric: Appropriations of Ancient Discourse*. Hillsdale: Lawrence Erlbaum Associates, 1990.

– – –. "Reconfiguring Writing and Delivery in Secondary Orality." *Rhetorical Memory and Delivery*, ed. John Frederick Reynolds. Hillsdale: Lawrence Erlbaum Associates, 1993. 17–30.

Whately, Richard. *Elements of Rhetoric*. London: Longmans, 1877.

Wixon, Vincent, and Pat Wixon. "Using Talk–Write in the Classroom." *Theory and Practice in the Teaching of Composition: Processing, Distancing and Modeling*, eds. Miles Myers and James Gray. Urbana: NCTE, 1983. 129–35.

Yoos, George. "An Identity of Roles in Writing and Reading." *College Composition and Communication* 30 (October, 1979): 245–50.

Young, Richard E., Alton L. Becker, and Kenneth L. Pike. *Rhetoric: Discovery and Change*. New York: Harcourt Brace, 1970.

Zoellner, Robert. "Talk–Write: A Behavioral Pedagogy for Composition." *College English* 30 (January 1969): 267–320.

Suggested Readings

Anderson, Chris. "Dramatism and Deliberation." *Rhetoric Review* 3 (September 1985): 34–43.

Anson, Chris M., et al. *Scenarios for Teaching Writing: Contexts for Discussion and Reflexive Practice*. Urbana: NCTE, 1993.

Auer, Jeffrey J., and Jerald L. Banninga. "The Genesis of John Quincy Adams' Lectures on Rhetoric and Oratory." *Quarterly Journal of Speech* 44 (1963): 119–32.

Austin, Gilbert. "From Chironomia." *The Rhetorical Tradition*, eds. Patricia Bizzell and Bruce Herzberg. Boston: St. Martin's, 1990. 739–45.

Baldwin, Charles Sears. *Composition, Oral and Written*. New York: Longmans, 1909.

Bartholomae, David. "Inventing the University." *When a Writer Can't Write*, ed. Mike Rose. New York: Guilford, 1985.

Bates, Jeffrey. *Writing Out Loud*. Reston: Acropolis, 1990.

Belanger, Kelly, et al. "Gender and Writing: Biblio(bio)graphical Stories." *Rhetoric Society Quarterly* 20.4 (Fall, 1990): 367–401.

Berlin, James. *Rhetoric and Reality*. Carbondale: Southern Illinois UP, 1987.

Berthoff, Ann E. *The Making of Meaning. Metaphors, Models and Maxims for Writing Teachers*. Upper Montclair: Boynton, 1981.

Blankenship, J., and H. G. Stelzner. *Rhetoric and Communication*. Urbana: University of Illinois Press, 1976.

Bowersock, G. W. *Greek Sophists in the Roman Empire*. Oxford: Clarendon, 1969.

Brink, J. R., ed. *Female Scholars: A Tradition of Learned Women Before 1800*. Montreal: Eden Press Women's Publications, 1980.

Buck, Gertrude. *A Handbook of Argumentation and Debating*. Orange: The Orange Chronicle, 1906.

– – –. "The Present Status of Rhetorical Theory." *Modern Language Notes* 15 (1900): 167–74.

– – –. "Recent Tendencies in the Teaching of English Composition." *Educational Review* 22 (1901): 371–82.

– – –. "What Does 'Rhetoric' Mean?" *Educational Review* 22 (1901): 197–200.

– – –, and Kristine Mann. *A Course in Narrative Writing*. New York: Holt, 1906.

– – –, and Elisabeth Woodbridge. *A Course in Expository Writing*. (Morris). New York: Holt, 1899.

128 SUGGESTED READINGS

Burke, Rebecca J. *Gertrude Buck's Rhetorical Theory*. As part of a series, Occasional Papers in Composition History and Theory, no. 1, ed. Donald C. Stewart. Kansas State, 1978. 1–26.

Calder, Boni, et al. *Guide 1983–84*. ERIC ED 280017. 1987.

Carpenter, Carol. "Exercises to Combat Sexist Reading and Writing." *College English* 43 (1981): 293–300.

Casaregola, Vincent. *Declassicizing Ancient Rhetoric: Toward a Reconstructed Rhetoric of Oral Performance*. Paper presented at the Annual Meeting of CCCC. March, 1992. ERIC 348695. 1992.

Channing, Edward. *Lectures Read to Seniors in Harvard College, 1856*. Carbondale: Southern Illinois UP, 1968.

Cixous, Helene. "Aller a la Mer" [Going to the Seaside]. *Modern Drama* 27.4 (December 1984): 546–48.

Connolly, Francis. *A Rhetoric Case Book*. New York: Harcourt Brace, 1959.

Connors, Robert. "The Rhetoric of Explanation: Explanatory Rhetoric from 1850 to Present." *Written Communication* 2 (1985): 49–77.

—. "The Rise and Fall of the Modes of Discourse." *The Writing Teacher's Sourcebook*, eds. Gary Tate and Edward P. J. Corbett. Oxford: Oxford UP, 1981. 24–34.

Conway, Kathryn M. *Gertrude Buck, Rhetorician*. Paper presented at the Annual Meeting of CCCC, March, 1988. ERIC 296348. 1988.

Corbett, Edward P. J. *Classical Rhetoric for the Modern Student*. New York: Oxford UP, 1971.

Covino, William. *The Art of Wondering*. Portsmouth: Boynton, 1988.

Day, Henry Noble. *The Art of Discourse*. New York: Scribner, 1867.

de Pizan, Christine. *The Book of the City of Ladies*. New York: Persea, 1982.

deQuincey, Thomas. *Selected Essays on Rhetorical Education*, ed. Frederick Burwick, 1967.

Donawerth, Jane. "Bibliography of Women and the History of Rhetorical Theory to 1900." *Rhetoric Society Quarterly* 20.4 (Fall, 1990): 403–14.

duBois, Page. *Sowing the Body: Psychoanalysis and Ancient Representations of Women*. Chicago: University of Chicago Press, 1988.

Duhamel, Albert P. "The Function of Rhetoric in Effective Expression." *The Province of Rhetoric*, eds. Joseph Schwartz and John Rycenga. New York: Ronald, 1965. 36–48.

Dwyer, Evelyn M. *Enhancing Reading Comprehension through Creative Dramatics*. ERIC ED 316849. 1990.

Ehninger, Douglas. "A Synoptic View of Systems of Western Rhetoric." *Quarterly Journal of Speech* 61 (December, 1975): 448–53.

Ellis, Robert, ed. *Competition Monologues*. Lanham: UP of America, 1988.

Ellis, Robert, ed. *Competition Monologues II*. Lanham: UP of America, 1989.

Elshtain, Jean Bethke. *Public Man, Private Woman: Women in Social and Political Thought*. Princeton: Princeton UP, 1981.

Enos, Theresa. *Encyclopedia of Rhetoric and Composition*. New York: Garland, 1996.

—. "Reports of the 'Author's' Death May Be Greatly Exaggerated But the 'Writer' Lives on in the Text." *Rhetoric Society Quarterly* 20.4 (Fall, 1990): 339–45.

Eunapius. *Lives of the Philosophers and Sophists*, trans. Wilmer Cave Wright. Bound with Philostratus' *The Lives of the Sophists*. 1921. Cambridge, MA: Harvard UP, 1961. (pp. 399–419 on Sosipatra).

Ferguson, Moira, ed. *First Feminists*. Bloomington: Indiana UP, 1985.

Finnegan, Ruth. *Oral Poetry: Its Nature, Significance and Social Context*. Cambridge: Cambridge UP, 1977.

Fish, Stanley. *Is There a Text in This Class? The Authority of Interpretive Communities.* Cambridge, MA: Harvard UP, 1980.

Fisher, Walter R. *Human Communication as Narrative: Toward a Philosophy of Reason, Value, and Action.* Columbia: University of South Carolina Press, 1987.

Focus on Collaboration. Urbana: NCTE, 1988.

Fontaine, Sheryl I., and Susan Hunter, eds. *Writing Ourselves into the Story.* Carbondale: Southern Illinois UP, 1993.

Fulton, Robert, and Thomas Trueblood. *Practical Elements of Elocution.* New York: Ginn, 1893.

Gennette, Gerard. *Narrative Discourse: An Essay on Method,* trans. Jane E. Lewin. Ithaca, New York: Cornell UP, 1980.

Gere, Ann Ruggles. "Insights from the Blind: Composing without Revising." *Revising: New Essays for Teachers of Writing,* ed. Ronald A. Sudol. Urbana: NCTE, 1982. 52–70.

Glyn, Elinor. *The Elinor Glyn System of Writing,* Vol. 2–4. Auburn, New York: Authors' Press, 1922.

Golden, James L., and Edward P. J. Corbett. *The Rhetoric of Blair, Campbell, and Whately.* Carbondale: Southern Illinois UP, 1990.

Gunning, Robert. *The Technique of Clear Writing.* New York: McGraw-Hill, 1952.

Halloran, Michael S. "Rhetoric in the American College Curriculum: The Decline of Public Discourse." *Pre/Text* 3.3 (1982): 245–69.

Harkin, Patricia. "The Post-Disciplinary Politics of Lore." *Contending with Words: Composition and Rhetoric in a Postmodern Age,* eds. Patricia Harkin and John Schilb. New York: MLA, 1991.

Hart, Sophie C. "English in the College." *School Review* 10 (1902): 364–73.

Hayakawa, S. I. "Learning to Think and to Write: Semantics in Freshman English." *College Composition and Communication* 13.1 (1962): 5–8.

Hayes, Mary, ed. *Teachers and Writers: Articles from the Ohio Writing Project.* ERIC ED 232210. 1981.

Herreman, Dana. "None of Us Is as Smart as All of Us." *Focus on Collaboration.* Urbana: NCTE, 1988. 5–11.

Hikins, James. "Plato's Rhetorical Theory: Old Perspectives on the Epistemology of the New Rhetoric." *Central States Speech Journal* 32 (Fall 1981): 160–76.

Hill, Adams Sherman. *The Principles of Rhetoric.* Cincinnati: American Book, 1895.

Horner, Winifred. "The Roots of Modern Writing Instruction: Eighteenth- and Nineteenth-Century Britain." *Rhetoric Review* 8.2 (Spring, 1990): 322–45.

Horner, Winifred Bryan, ed. *Composition and Literature: Bridging the Gap.* University of Chicago Press, 1983.

Howe, Tina. "Painting Churches." *Monologues: Women 3,* eds. Robert Emerson and Jane Grumbach. New York: Drama Book Publishers, 1989.

Hughes, Richard. "The Contemporaneity of Classical Rhetoric." *College Composition and Communication* 16 (1965): 158–59.

Irigaray, Luce. *This Sex Which is Not One.* Ithaca: Cornell UP, 1985.

Jarratt, Susan. *Rereading the Sophists: Classical Rhetoric Refigured.* Carbondale: Southern Illinois UP, 1991.

Johnson, Nan. "*Ethos* and the Aims of Rhetoric." *Essays on Classical Rhetoric and Modern Discourse,* eds. Robert Connors, Lisa Ede, and Andrea Lunsford. Carbondale: Southern Illinois UP, 1984.

Jordan, Mary A. *Correct Writing and Speaking.* The Woman's Home Library Series. New York: Barnes, 1904.

Kantor, Kenneth J., and Donald L. Rubin. "Between Speaking and Writing: Processes of Differentiation." *Exploring Speaking-Writing Relationships*, eds. Barry M. Kroll and Robert J. Vann. Urbana: NCTE, 1981. 55–81.

Keller, Frank, and Charles Brown. "An Interpersonal Ethic for Communication." *Journal of Communication* 16 (1968): 73–81.

Kennedy, George. *The Art of Rhetoric in the Roman World*. Princeton: Princeton UP, 1972.

– – –. *Greek Rhetoric Under Christian Emperors*. Princeton, NJ: Princeton UP, 1983.

Kidd, Robert. *A Rhetorical Reader for Class Drill and Private Instruction in Elocution*. Cincinnati: Wilson, Hinkle & Co., 1870.

Kinneavy, James. "Restoring the Humanities: The Return of Rhetoric from Exile." *The Rhetorical Tradition and Modern Writing*, ed. James J. Murphy. New York: MLA, 1982. 19–28.

– – –. *A Theory of Discourse*. New York: Norton, 1971.

Kirkham, Samuel. *English Grammar in Familiar Lectures*. New York: Collins, 1829.

Knoblauch, C. H., and Lil Brannon. *The Rhetorical Tradition and the Teaching of Writing*. Upper Montclair: Boynton, 1984.

Knodt, Ellen Andrews. "If at First You Don't Succeed: Effective Strategies for Teaching Composition in the Two-Year College." *Two-Year College English: Essays for a New Century*, ed. Mark Reynolds. Urbana: NCTE, 1994.

Labalme, Patricia H., ed. *Beyond Their Sex: Learned Women of the European Past*. New York: New York UP, 1980.

Lamb, Catherine E. "Beyond Argument in Feminist Composition." *College Composition and Communication* 42 (1991): 11–24.

Leff, Michael. "In Search of Ariadne's Thread." *Central State Speech Journal* 29 (Summer 1978): 73–91.

Lindemann, Erika. *A Rhetoric for Writing Teachers*. New York: Oxford UP, 1982.

Lockwood, Sara, and Mary Alice Emerson. *Composition and Rhetoric for Higher Schools*. Boston: Ginn, 1901. Revised ed. *Composition and Rhetoric*. 1912.

Lunsford, Andrea, and Lisa Ede. *Singular Texts/Plural Authors: Perspectives on Collaborative Writing*. Carbondale: Southern Illinois UP, 1990.

Macdonell, Diane. *Theories of Discourse: An Introduction*. Oxford: Blackwell, 1986.

Macrorie, Ken. *Telling Writing*. 3rd ed. Rochelle Park: Hayden, 1981.

Marks, Elaine, and Isabelle de Courtivron, eds. *New French Feminisms*. Amherst: University of Massachusetts Press, 1980.

Marrou, Henri I. *The Meaning of History*, trans. Robert J. Olsen. Baltimore: Helicon, 1966.

Martin, Theodora Penny. *The Sound of Our Own Voices*. Boston: Beacon, 1987.

McGuffey's Newly Revised Rhetorical Guide. Cincinnati: Wilson, Hinkle & Co., 1865.

Miller, Thomas P. *Reinventing the Rhetorical Tradition*. Paper presented at CCCC, Chicago, March, 1990.

Morgan, Anna. *The Art of Speech and Development*. Chicago: McClurg, 1909.

Mulderig, Gerald. "Gertrude Buck's Rhetorical Theory and Modern Composition Teaching." *Rhetoric Society Quarterly* 14 (1984): 96–104.

Murphy, James J. "The Modern Value of Ancient Roman Methods of Teaching Writing, with Answers to Twelve Current Fallacies." *Writing on the Edge* 1.1: 28–37.

– – –, ed. *Renaissance Eloquence: Studies in the Theory and Practice of Renaissance Rhetoric*. Berkeley: University of California Press, 1983.

– – –. *The Rhetorical Tradition and Modern Writing*. New York: MLA, 1982.

Myers, Greg. "Reality, Consensus, and Reform in the Rhetoric of Composition Teaching." *College English* 48 (1986): 154–74.

Newkirk, Thomas. "Barrett Wendell's Theory of Discourse." *Rhetoric Review* 10.1 (Fall, 1991): 20–30.

Norton, James H., and Francis Gretton. *Writing Incredibly Short Plays, Poems, Stories.* New York: Harcourt Brace, 1972.

Ohmann, Richard. "Speech Acts and the Definition of Literature." *Philosophy and Rhetoric* 4.1 (1984): 1–19.

Olsen, David R. "From Utterance to Text: The Bias of Language in Speech and Writing." *Harvard Educational Review* 47 (August 1977): 257–81.

O'Neill, Cecily, and Alan Lambert. *Drama Structures: A Practical Handbook for Teachers.* London: Hutchinson, 1985.

O'Neill, R. H., and N. M. Boretz. *The Director as Artist: Play Direction Today.* New York: Holt, 1987.

Ong, Walter. *Ramus, Method and the Decay of Dialogue.* Cambridge, MA: Harvard UP, 1958.

Parker, William Riley. "Where Do English Departments Come From?" *The Writing Teacher's Sourcebook*, eds. Gary Tate and Edward P. J. Corbett. Oxford: Oxford UP, 1981. 3–15.

Peaden, Catherine. "Feminist Theories, Historiographies and Histories of Rhetoric: The Role of Feminism in Historical Studies." *Rhetoric and Ideology: Compositions and Criticisms of Power*, ed. Charles W. Kneuper. Arlington, TX: Rhetoric Society of America, 1989. 116–26.

Poulakos, John. "Toward a Sophistic Definition of Rhetoric." *Philosophy and Rhetoric* 16 (1983): 35–48.

Presnell, Michael. "Narrative Gender Differences: Orality and Literacy." *Doing Research on Women's Communication: Perspectives on Theory and Method*, eds. Kathryn Carter and Carole Spitzack. Norwood: Ablex, 1989.

Quackenbos, George Payn. *A Course of Composition and Rhetoric.* New York: Appleton, 1854.

Ramsey, Allen. "Rhetoric and the Ethics of 'Seeming.'" *Rhetoric Society Quarterly* 11.2 (Spring 1981): 85–96.

Ramus, Peter. "Arguments in Rhetoric Against Quintilian." *The Rhetorical Tradition*, eds. Patricia Bizzell and Bruce Herzberg. Boston: St. Martin's, 1990. 563–83.

Randolph, Karen. "Oral and Written Discourse: From Talking to Writing." *Teachers and Writers: Articles from the Ohio Writing Project*, ed. Mary Hayes. ERIC ED 232210. 1981.

Reid, Ronald F. "The Boyleston Professorship of Rhetoric and Oratory, 1806–1904: A Case Study in Changing Concepts of Rhetoric and Pedagogy." *Quarterly Journal of Speech* 45 (1959): 239–57.

Reynolds, Mark, ed. *Two-Year College English: Essays for a New Century.* Urbana: NCTE, 1994.

Rouse, Joy. "Positional Historiography and Margaret Fuller's Public Discourse of Mutual Interpretation." *Rhetoric Society Quarterly* 20.3 (Summer 1990): 233–39.

Russell, David R. *Writing in the Academic Disciplines, 1870–1990.* Southern Illinois UP, 1991.

Scott, Fred Newton. "English Composition as a Mode of Behavior." *English Journal* 11 (1922): 463–73.

Scott, Robert L. "On Viewing Rhetoric as Epistemic." *Central States Speech Journal* (1967): 9–17.

– – –. "A Synoptic View of Systems of Western Rhetoric." *Quarterly Journal of Speech* 61 (December, 1975): 439–47.

Searing, Annie E. P. "Why College Graduates Are Deficient in English." *Educational Review* 16 (1898): 244–53.

Secor, Marie. "The Legacy of Nineteenth-Century Style Theory." *Rhetoric Society Quarterly* 22 (Spring 1982): 76–84.

Shipley, Joseph T. *Playing With Words.* Englewood Cliffs: Prentice-Hall, 1965.

Shoemaker, Rachel, ed. *Classical Dialogues and Dramas*. Philadelphia: Penn, 1888.

Simons, Sarah E., and Clem Irwin Orr. *Dramatization: Selections from English Classics Adapted in Dramatic Form*. Chicago: Scott, 1913.

Southwick, Jessie (née Eldridge). *The Emerson Philosophy of Expression; an Application to Character Education*. Boston: Expression, 1930.

Sprague, Rosamond Kent, ed. *The Older Sophists: A Complete Translation by Several Hands of the Fragments in Die Fragmente der Vorsokratiker*, eds. Diels-Kranz and published by Weidmann Verlag. Columbia: University of South Carolina Press, 1972.

Stewart, Donald. "Some History Lessons for Composition Teachers." *The Writing Teacher's Sourcebook*, eds. Gary Tate and Edward P. J. Corbett. Oxford: Oxford UP, 1981. 16–23.

Sutherland, Christine Mason. "Outside the Rhetorical Tradition: Mary Astell's Advice to Women in Seventeenth-Century England." *Rhetoric* 9.2 (Spring 1991): 147–63.

Swearingen, Jan C. "Literate Rhetors and Their Illiterate Audiences: The Orality of Early Literacy." *PRE/TEXT* 7 (1986): 145–62.

Tanner, William M. *Composition and Rhetoric*. New York: Ginn, 1922.

Tate, Gary, ed. *Teaching Composition: Twelve Bibliographical Essays*. Fort Worth: Texas Christian UP, 1987.

Theremin, Francis. *Eloquence a Virtue: An Outline of A Systematic Rhetoric*, trans. W.G.T. Shedd. Philadelphia: Smith, 1859.

Tobin, Lad, and Thomas Newkirk, eds. *Taking Stock: The Writing Process Movement in the '90s*. Portsmouth: Boynton, 1994.

Tompkins, Jane. "Pedagogy of the Distressed." *College English* 52 (October 1990): 653–60.

Treadway, Cheryl. "Using Field Work to Teach Writing." *Teachers and Writers: Articles from the Ohio Writing Project*, ed. Mary Hayes. ERIC ED 232210. 1981.

Trimbur, John. "Consensus and Difference in Collaborative Learning." *College English* 51 (1989): 602–16.

Uchmanowicz, Pauline. *The History of Rhetoric and Composition as Cultural Studies*. Paper presented at the Annual Meeting of MLA. December, 1993. ERIC ED 375431. 1993.

Vatz, Richard. "The Myth of the Rhetorical Situation." *Philospohy and Rhetoric* 6 (1972): 154–61.

Walker, John. *Elements of Elocution*. Boston: Mallory, 1781.

– – –. *A Rhetorical Grammar*. London: Robinson, 1787.

Wallace, Karl. *Understanding Discourse: The Speech Act and Rhetorical Action*. Baton Rouge: Louisiana State UP, 1970.

Warren, Helen B. *The Absence of Women from the History of Rhetoric: Exclusion or Omission?* Paper presented at the Annual Meeting of the Eastern Communication Association, April 27–May 1, 1988. ERIC ED 294287. 1988.

Weaver, Richard M. "The *Phaedrus* and the Nature of Rhetoric." *The Ethics of Rhetoric*. South Bend: Gateway, 1953. 50–62.

Wise, J. Hooper. *College English: The First Year*. New York: Harcourt Brace, 1956.

Wixon, Vincent, and Pat Stone. "Getting It Out, Getting It Down: Adapting Zoellner's Talk–Write." *English Journal* 66 (1977): 70–73.

Woolley, Edwin C. *New Handbook of Composition*. New York: Heath, 1926.

Yoos, George. "A Revision of the Concept of Ethical Appeal." *Philosophy and Rhetoric* 12 (Winter, 1979): 41–58.

Author Index

Subject Index